COMMENDATION

Here is another in Lady Cassidi's series of prayer and experience. She has gathered th acquaintances over many years. I hope you have done. Hardly a question is not addressed and answered – indeed I wonder if anyone can do without it!

Annie Maw
Lord Lieutenant of Somerset

Editor's foreword.
Firstly I would like to thank the busy friends David Owen, Victoria Glendinning, Jenny Barraclough and John Tydeman, James Crowden poet extraordinary and the late and much missed David Rutherford, gifted vintner, for their contributions; my granddaughter Lizzy for the front cover illustration and the many friends who have delved into their memories and archives for their Useful Tips. My thanks, too, to Liz Jones who spent many hours typing and organising the text, the members of Pitney Parish Church and Sarah Cox in the Langport Church Office who put the final touches to the book and finally to my husband Desmond, without whom the book would not have been possible.

How to use the book
The main sections of the book are arranged in alphabetical order as are the subsections with the exception of those in the section How to be a Good--- where Agriculture, Armed Forces, Church, etc. professions are each grouped together. Individual names of contributors have not been given but indications of professions or employment are given in italics without brackets and Editorial comments are in (italics with brackets.) Potentially life-saving tips are given in red.

Sadly I have not been able to try all the tips advised in the book so please forgive me if that stubborn stain goes red instead of disappearing, the bees sting you or you don't achieve that perfect painting.

INDEX

Arts and Crafts	Page 4
Beauty	Page 9
Cooking and Food Hygiene	Page 11
DIY	Page 17
Education	Page 19
Field Sports	Page 20
Finances	Page 23
Gardening	Page 25
Health and First Aid	Page 32
Hobbies	Page 41
Hospitality	Page 47
Household	Page 50
How To....	Page 63
How To Be A Good...	Page 66
Humour	Page 84
Moving House	Page 88
Relationships	Page 92
Speaking and Writing Skills	Page 95
Sport	Page 97
Travel and Holidays	Page 100
Travelling and Driving	Page 104

ACKNOWLEDGEMENTS

Many thanks to all the stores, brands and many friends who have helped us financially with the production of this book:
Croydex
John Lewis
Kelly Fletcher of Jolly Red
Monkton Elm Garden Centre
Overt Locke
Rohan Clothes
Wolf Tools

General Advice

"Never assume anything." *given by a head teacher who, with her husband who is a surgeon, was working in the besieged city of Sarajevo. They reached the last plane to leave the city by running down the runway criss-crossed by sniper fire.*
Do fewer things well.
Leave time to stand and stare.
To find out how to do any complex new task watch it on YouTube.

Life in general: If you are doing something wrong stop at once *(advice from a well known writer).*

A lady never takes offence.

For any task. Familiarise yourself with the internet. Look at the film on YouTube for actions taken.
If you don't find the answer, look for a forum for worldwide expert advice. A forum is particularly useful for information on non-active tasks. Be as particular as possible, e.g. if studying the Tudors for GCSE History, put in "The Tudors schools standard". This saves being swamped with information. If one word doesn't work, try another.

ARTS AND CRAFTS

Dressmaking

Measure twice, cut once. If working from a pattern, write measurement of person on pattern – bust or hip size may not be standard.
Start with a simple pattern and plain fabric. Check length of skirt and trousers before cutting.
Press all seams as you go along. If inserting a zip in centre of back or front do this first while fabric is flat. Tack seams and try for fit before finishing. Avoid anything on the bias.
Double check that the nap on patterned material is the same way.
For velvet the nap is smooth in one direction and rough in the other (feel with hand). Make sure the nap is in the same direction and for skirts have the sheen (the downward facing nap) facing down i.e. it is smooth when you sweep your hand over it.
For curved seams such as joining in sleeve or neckband pin and tack first.
If sight is a difficulty use a crewel needle and a needle threader available at haberdashers and a daylight bulb.

Embroidery

When binding the inner ring of an embroidery frame use 2"/4mm non stretch bandage. This makes the task very easy. A square of cling film stretched over the non working area of your work will ensure that it stays clean.
There is a stitching book available for left-handed embroiderers (Amazon).
To avoid knots and twisting of your threads when using stranded silk on cotton separate the threads before using them. Always use an embroidery needle size 8 or 9 – small is best. If in doubt about stitching etc, consult YouTube.

Knitting

Choose a good pattern and the best available wool. (But if knitting for a fast growing child and on a budget then cheaper wool might be all right.) Buy plenty of wool of the same dye lot. Dye lots can vary a lot in hue. Read the washing and ironing instructions on the wool band and keep one band for future reference.

Knitting the tension square shown on the pattern is well worth it. It only takes 10 mins. to knit a square of 10 stitches x 10 rows. This show what tension <u>you</u> work at. If the tension is too loose use smaller needles. The pattern will also tell you how many yards of wool will be used. When starting to cast on leave enough wool end to start joining the seam.

Wool can be ironed but <u>never</u> use a steam iron. When ready to assemble the garment spread the pieces on a table, abutt the edges and join with a running stitch. Use the length of wool left when work is first cast on.

With mohair wool keep the wool in the fridge. This stops you getting covered in hair. For arthritic hands use <u>wooden</u> needles. Polish them with furniture polish to make them slide easily. *(Advice given by a consultant rheumatologist.)* For heavy garments use a circular needle and simply turn the work around at end of each row.

Wash the garment before wearing. (Advice on washing wool is in the Household section.)

Patchwork and quilting

Measure twice and cut once.

When making a quilt such as a bed quilt that will need occasional washing make sure that all the fabrics are washable e.g. don't use velvet and cotton or woollen fabric with cotton. When using felt all the patches must be felt.

Quilting

When making a patchwork quilted item make sure that the patchwork top is finished before buying the wadding backing. When making a quilt from a pattern check whether the pattern does or does not allow for seams.

Sewing

Use the old adage "A stitch in time saves nine". Make sure that hands are clean before starting.

Have a magnet in sewing basket. Get a good sewing manual.

Sewing needle: Cut end with good sharp scissors. The best needle threaders are the simple wire ones. The sharpest scissors are those for button holing.

Use sharp pins and throw away blunt or damaged ones. Use gold pins for fine fabrics.
Check buttonhole size before and immediately before finishing.
For sewing name tapes on socks put a wine bottle inside the sock before sewing.
Multi-purpose nametapes: If two or three children are involved put initials of each child on the same tape starting with the eldest first, e.g. JM, AC, WR Smith.
When stitching, take a tuck to hide the intermediaries or cut off the redundant ones.
In the 1980's an undergraduate took a midnight dip in the fountain of a famous quad. The first thing her mother knew about this was a phone call from her daughter saying angrily, "Mum, how <u>dare</u> you leave the name tapes on my underwear."
Buying a sewing machine: Choose a well known make whose parts will not go out of date. Choose one where the spool is the standard one not the shuttle type. Standard spools are easily loaded and more can be purchased to store with different colours.
Gutermann threads are stronger than Coats. The large cheap reels are fine for tacking but do not wear so well and may break in the machine. Dark and pale green threads blend in well with a variety of colours. Take advice from your local merchant and ask for a comprehensive lesson.
Take notes during lesson. Keep the instruction manuals safely as the instructions are forgotten especially for attachments. When threading machine needle hold a white card behind the hole in the needle and use a needle threader if necessary.
When machining set machine at a large stitch length e.g. 7 or 8. It will ride over pins set at right angles to the machine but beware with smaller stitches as needle may easily break.
When finishing a line of stitching a few stitches in reverse will secure the end. Always pull more of the upper thread through the needle before cutting it. This will prevent unthreading the needle.
Sewing repairs and alterations:
To change length of trousers: Wear trousers to try length. Allow 1½" to 2" plus ½" turn over for normal trousers and ¾"+ turnover for jeans. Keep all scraps from trousers for patching later. Patching: Allow plenty of material. Pin and tack first. Turning frayed shirt collar: easiest unpicked. Turn and pin

and tack then stitch collar only. Turning with the band will be harder as a new buttonhole is needed. **Sides to middle on an old sheet**: Use run and fell seam (see illustration) if edges frayed. If not frayed, simply lay sides on top of each other as shown.

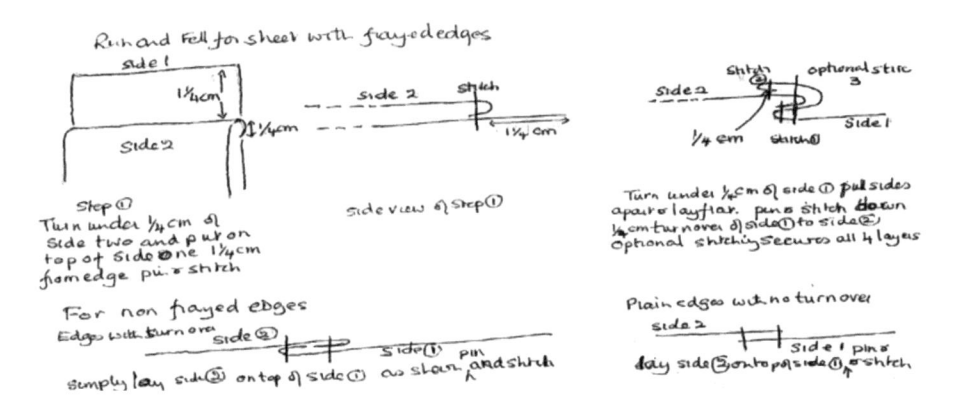

[Illustration: Run and Fell for sheet with frayed edges, showing side 1, side 2, stitch positions with measurements 1¼ cm and ¼ cm. Step ①: Turn under ¼ cm of side two and put on top of side one 1¼ cm from edge plus stitch. Side view of Step ①. For non-frayed edges: edges with turn over side ②, simply lay side ② on top of side ① as shown and stitch. Also shown: Turn under ¼ cm of side ①, pull sides apart, lay flat, pins stitch down ¼ cm, turn over side ① to side ②, optional stitching secures all 4 layers. Plain edges with no turn over side 2, side 1 pins, lay side ② onto pins side ①, stitch.]

Tapestry
More correctly known as canvas work.
This can seem to be a complicated hobby so the best bet is to get a canvas with a design on it from a reputable firm such as, 'Jolly Red' which gives excellent and clear instructions.
Use a square or rectangular frame. The only additional tips are: The rudimentary one – to thread the wool on the tapestry needle bend the wool over the end of the needle with the hole, pull tight and slide the needle out. You are then left with a manageable fold of wool which can be pressed easily through the hole. Measure its destination and the canvas twice before choosing a canvas.
For the background get ample wool of the same dye lot – not so vital for flowers where variations will not show. Sort the colours in daylight. Don't start in a corner. For a picture a smooth back is essential – no knots: not so important for soft furnishings.

Upholstery
Make sure that the frame of the chair is clear of tacks, that holes are filled with wood filler and that joints are sound. Treat for woodworm if required and take a photo before starting.

Write down the sequence of work and check that all materials are to hand. Make sure that the old horse hair is washed in a pillowcase well in advance. Be very careful tightening the calico as it stretches.
For the fabric, choose one that will not show dirt easily, that does not fray easily and that the pattern fits with the shape of the chair. Use Uhu glue to put on braid.

Picture Framing *given by a local picture framer*
When choosing a frame, select one that provides enough strength. The colour of the frame should be no darker than the darkest part of the picture or lighter than the lightest part.
Remember that dark colours reflect more behind glass so consider anti-reflective glass. Museum glass blocks 98% of UV light which fades colours. When hanging pictures they should be at eye level or 160cm from the floor. For low ceilings hanging pictures too high will make the ceilings appear even lower. To prevent the back of a picture from getting damp (especially watercolours) cut slivers of wine corks 3mm thick and stick one on the back of each bottom corner of the picture to ensure the back does not touch the wall. Watercolours should be kept out of sunlight to prevent fading. Picture framing is available in House of Talbot in Langport and Wot a Picture in Street.

Making Shell Pictures and Picture frames
Frames made by children: cover a frame with Polyfilla and embed shells in the desired pattern.
Elaborate pictures with small shells *(given by an expert's daughter)*: This craft was first developed in Boston then taught in Bermuda where the contributor's family learnt the craft. For large, elaborate pictures; first collect a lot of small shells then draw the design and place the shells on the design then transfer to pieces of cork which can be glued to the board. For small pictures and little boxes glue directly onto the surface.

BEAUTY

Beauty *given by a Langport beautician*
Keep healthy and eat well, using a balanced diet and do not over eat. A balanced diet can be judged by spreading out the week's food – physically or in the mind's eye. If there is a wide range of colours it is a healthy diet. If the colours are monochrome and dull it is unhealthy and mainly carbohydrate.
Protect the skin from the sun using a good sun cream. Sunlight causes immediate damage to the skin as well as causing skin cancer.
Smoking causes premature ageing of the skin – it is the demolition waiting to happen.
Clean the skin every night. Make-up gives some protection from dirt and damaging substances in the air but should be removed with a cleansing cream which, unlike soap and water, does not dry the skin. To prevent skin ageing choose a medium priced product so as not to pay for the advertising. Young skin can tolerate a cheaper product.
Teenage Beauty This jingle used to be said at an open window at Benenden Girls' Boarding School in the post-war era and in other girls' schools. The hands are clenched and the shoulders are taken back hard in time with the jingle.

I must, I must, I must.
I must improve my bust.
The bigger the better, the tighter the sweater,
The boys depend on us.

Nails: to avoid splitting nails: keep nails short so that they are less likely to break off. After cutting use a metal file followed by a fine emery file. Test for snagging on a fleece material.
Keep nails as dry as possible by wearing rubber gloves when possible. Take zinc to strengthen nail. Try a commercial nail strengthener. There is a range of them made by Sally Hansen available at Boots.
If a crack goes into the nail bed: cut as close as possible and file, then cover it with plaster till it grows out (may take 1 to 2 weeks).
Hand cream: Use aqueous cream or the following recipe. Put some calendula flower petals in olive oil and leave for 4-6 weeks in a sealed jar on a sunny window ledge. Strain and add a little lavender oil. Mix with beeswax 60% oil

and 40% beeswax (bees' wax).
If a tube of hand cream seems empty, cut off the bottom to get a lot more. *(Might work for tooth paste, make up etc?)*
Make-up bag: Keep everything in the bag as small as possible e.g. Bourjois healthy mix instead of a powder compact if you can manage without a mirror. Include small container of Amplex and of cough sweets (e.g. Imps). Sharp nail scissors are useful for many eventualities, as are tweezers. The flat handle of a metal nail file will serve as an emergency knife for spreading and as a screwdriver. Then, of course, add eye make-up, lipstick and mascara.

Care of hair *given by a Langport hairdresser*
Have your hair cut regularly by a good hairdresser. No DIY! Use a shampoo that suits your hair. People often confuse dandruff and flakes from a dry scalp. Dandruff is itchy and the flakes are yellow. Dry scalp gives white flakes.

For Protection from Ageing: see advice under suntan cream in Travel and Holidays.

COOKING AND FOOD HYGIENE

Cooking
Use more wine.
Clear away one task before embarking on another.
When cooking a roast meal cook more potatoes and make more gravy than you expect to use. Leftover gravy can be added to soup, also any residual juice. When clearing up add a little water to the pan and heat on top of the oven then add to soup. Use vegetable water and wine to make the gravy.
Macaroni cheese: add a teaspoon of mustard to enhance the flavour.
Mince pies: pierce the bottom with a fork to stop pastry rising and pushing out the mince.
Blind baking: Use cling film instead of dry beans.
Slice lemon and keep in a jar in the freezer ready to put into drinks.
To remove frozen cheesecake from aluminium container: Clip vertically round the edge of the foil about 2 cm at a time with secateurs. Cut right down with a sharp knife. Fold each section down. Slide/lift pudding off with slice or large knife. This must be done while still frozen.
To stop onions causing tears when being chopped, keep damp cloths nearby and wipe hands frequently.   Get parsley into a tight bundle and chop with scissors directly where needed.
Whizz stale bread in a blender then freeze as breadcrumbs, you can add parsley for future use.
Always keep lemons in the house. They enhance most things, e.g. chicken, stewed apple, etc.
To tell a raw egg from a well boiled egg, spin round on a table. Raw eggs will not spin whereas well boiled eggs will. To keep coffee grounds fresh keep in fridge.
Unruly cling film. Use the type with perforations to tear off individual sheets. These can be purchased at Lakeland.
To clean new potatoes: Use Lady Jane fine cleaning pads.
To keep the vitamins in potatoes: When cooking potatoes be aware that most of the vitamins are stored just below the skin. New potatoes are therefore best left in their skins. If larger potatoes are cooked use as good a peeler as possible or remove skins after cooking. They then come off leaving

the layer containing the vitamins behind. Research has found that mashing is more destructive of vitamins than any other process.

To stop milk sticking to pans put a tiny bit of milk in the pan first.

Keep the seal of a plastic milk bottle and put in the lid to stop leakage when flat.

Use a rubber scraper with a sharp edge not a blunt one.

Bread crumbs: Put in low oven and harden off for dog biscuits.

To keep cheese fresh, buy a cotton cheese bag from a good provider and keep in the bottom of the fridge. (*It really works.*)

To stop avocados from going brown in a salad, leave the stone in the bowl. Cover bowl with cling film. Remove before adding dressing and serving.

To top and tail gooseberries: Freeze, then rub ends off while still frozen.

For cucumber sandwiches, try a thin layer of Marmite instead of salt.

To keep celery crisp either stand up in a jug of water or perhaps better – wrap in silver foil and keep in the fridge.

Removing jam pot and other lids:

Put boiling water in a saucer. Invert the pot and steep in the water for 30 seconds then remove lid. (*The metal expands*)

Tap sharply round the edge of the lid with a hammer or wooden spoon.

Use multiple lid opener (Boa opener available at Overt Locke, Somerton – they also stock a number of mobility and assisted living aids)

To remove small lid, use door jamb as vice to grip lid.

To shell quail's eggs: When boiled cool in cold water, crack one end and run a coffee spoon between the shell and the egg.

To remove fat from the top of a hot stew: spread a sheet of kitchen roll onto the top till full of fat. Repeat till all fat removed and put the oily paper in the compost.

Cover Shreddies with olive oil, season, add to mixed nuts and heat – delicious! An American/Canadian variant: add pretzels to the above. This is known as "nuts and bolts".

Salt: To keep salt in a salt-cellar dry add a few grains of rice.

Recipes

Assemble all ingredients especially for baking before embarking on a task.

If a recipe is not satisfactory e.g. too salty, oven temp too high, make a pencil note in recipe book for next time.

Thai Rice for 4: To serve with Asian or European food – delicious!
8 cups cooked white rice. 2 tbs finely chopped deep fried garlic. 4 eggs. 1 ½ tbs light soy sauce
1 tsp sugar¼ cup vegetable oil: sliced cucumber and finely chopped spring onion to garnish
In a wok bring oil to high heat. Add eggs, stirring briskly until done, then add rice and stir over the heat until thoroughly mixed. Add soy sauce, and sugar, stirring until mixed in and the rice is heated through. Remove from heat, place on a hot serving dish and cover with the garlic and spring onion, place the cucumber around the edges to decorate.
For **Chinese stew** – use sliced cauliflower stalk instead of sliced bamboo shoots.
Scrambled eggs: Use a non-stick pan. To save utensils melt ample butter in a little milk in the pan add salt and pepper then break the eggs directly into the pan stirring each one vigorously as it is added. Addition of ready prepared chopped parsley enhances the taste. Do not overcook. The mixture should be mainly egg and butter, not pale yellow beads floating in a watery juice. Put directly onto hot buttered toast.
Omelettes: A variation on the normal with Spanish omelette. Separate the eggs and beat whites stiff with hand beater. Add the yolks, salt and pepper. Tip into hot butter in pan. Add filler. Wild Chanterelle mushrooms are particularly delicious.
White sauce without tears: Preheat the milk in a separate pan and add all at once to roux and stir. It will not form lumps and can be stirred with a wooden spoon.
Beaters: Effective beaters for gravy or egg white are the wire loop ones

A standard hand beater with ratchet and rotating side handle may be used but is more difficult to wash and store. Sharper knives are safer than blunt knives because they do not slip. To sharpen knives keep the blade as flat as possible to the steel or sharpening block. For knives with a bevelled edge use a knife sharpener.

When picking **elderflowers** in May go as early as possible on a fine morning before the little beetles get there and spoil your cordial. To get a richer cordial, before straining off the fruit, smash the fruit hard with the end of a rolling pin to extract the juice.

Easy Marmalade: Use one tin of Mamade, make up with orange juice not water. Continue as directed using a mixture of granulated and jam or preserving sugar. Add one tablespoon of black treacle to add darkness and interest.

Fruit cake: Use a heaped tablespoon of rough chopped marmalade instead of chopped peel. To stop burning put 3 layers of newspaper under greaseproof paper in the bottom of the tin. Surround the tin with 3 layers of newspaper tied in with string (tied in a bow). Paper should come 1cm above level of tin. Cover over top with more paper. Keep paper and string from year to year.

Jam making: Add a knob of butter to jam before it boils to stop frothing. To make strawberry jam set, use jam making sugar, not preserving sugar which is to keep jellies clear. Heat a small bowl of gooseberries (the amount that would just cover the bottom of a large pan) or red currants until very mushy and add to the strawberries.

Sandwiches: Butter the edges of the bread and the centre will butter itself. To remove crusts stack the sandwiches in the same order as the loaf. Press down with flat of hand and remove all crusts at same time. Not enough slices? One more can be made by putting the last crust flat on a board, crust up. Press down with flat of hand and saw across slice with bread knife.

WW2 austerity treat: Put a rich tea, or any other biscuit between two slices of bread. It's the difference in texture that makes it so delicious. It doesn't even need butter. *These were given to the editor when aged 9 at teatime or when sheltering under the stairs during an air raid.*

Another **easy and delicious recipe**: Mix 2 tbs harissa paste, 2 tbs yoghurt and 3tbs olive oil with salt and pepper. Marinate four chicken legs in a tightly fitting dish with the mixture spread on top. Bake in a hot oven and serve with rice and chutney. *(Wonderful bay tree chutneys can be obtained in Williams supermarket Somerton)*

A **quick pudding**: Hot cooked fruit (rhubarb, apples or pears), covered with broken up chocolate brownies. Add cream.

Freezing
For vegetables: Scald then drain through sieve/colander. Cool immediately with cold water, drain and dry with clean drying up cloth before bagging.
To bag up fruit or vegetables for freezing: label bag before filling then turn bag inside out, put in your hand, and grasp the first handful to make the rest of the filling easier or put fruit/vegetables into small dish and empty dish into bag. Working over a tray prevents escapers rolling onto the floor.

Wine *given by a retired wine merchant*
To clean a decanter: Drop two tablets of Steradent in the decanter; fill with warm water and leave overnight. Rinse and dry (*or put a little sharp sand in the decanter with some water, swill it around then wash and dry*).
Any red wine will improve if decanted, i.e. aerated. If wine is a little hard or unsympathetic, pour half a small glass of warm water into the decanter and pour the wine on top. It will improve it.
When buying wines, take a wine merchant's advice but stress your price bracket. Take his recommendations home and taste them with your family before buying in larger quantities.
Wine is a living product and improves if kept in a suitably cool place and lying down. This applies of course to red wine, but also to champagne, sparkling wines and fortified wines.
From a supermarket, fix your price bracket and style as you scan the shelves. Purchase one bottle of each wine selected and try it at home with food. When you have found one that you really enjoy at the right price, buy at least one case as they may sell out. Look out for special offers.
It is not always necessary to have red wine with meat and white wine with fish and poultry. Many people enjoy red wine with fish, especially in a sauce.
Pouring sparkling wine: have a glass ready; remove cover and wire; hold the cork firmly, covered with a cloth and twist the bottle from the base slowly to achieve minimum explosion.
Keep champagne fresh with a silver teaspoon. Do not store champagne bottles in the door of a fridge or if you must, then one only and beside the hinge. The hinges can break.
From a connoisseur of good wine
To **save a good wine** if only ½ bottle used, save up some ½ bottles and corks. Put leftover wine in small bottle and push cork in as far as possible. Hold

bottle with base against chest and bang cork against wall. Your body acts as a battering ram.

Kitchen Safety
Fly prevention: cover fruit with a fly net. Use old fashioned fly swot and fly papers or a UV fly zapper switched on at night. Chemical fly killers may be dangerous.

Have a fire extinguisher, fire blanket, first aid box and list of instructions in case of emergency in kitchen.
Include carbon monoxide (CO) detector (CO is not covered by a smoke alarm). Check CO detector and smoke alarm weekly. Symptoms of carbon monoxide poisoning (the silent killer) are **headache, dizziness, nausea, vomiting and shortness of breath**. It may mimic flu but there is no temperature. Skin colour is unreliable as it may vary from the classic rosy pink to blue/grey. The symptoms improve when away from the gas but will worsen the longer the exposure leading to loss of balance, vision and memory and can lead to loss of consciousness and be fatal within two hours. Treatment: evacuate and call 999. Free home safety visits are available for anyone over 55, under 78, or over 40 if living alone or a smoker; also any disabled person. Phone 0800 0502 999 for Devon and Somerset or look on www.dsfire.gov.uk
Nausea and vomiting may indicate food poisoning but there will be little or no diarrhoea.

DIY

Do It Yourself *(or, for some, Destroy It Yourself)*
How not to hit your thumb with a hammer: Do it twice and you won't do it again.
Do the most difficult part of a job first before getting tired.
To fill large gap between skirting board and wall: Make a narrow sausage of newspaper. Jam it into the gap and run filler over it. (DIY masters will, of course, remove and refit the board.)
Painting new wooden doors: Treat any knots with knotting solution before applying paint. Use good aluminium wood primer for outdoor work. Use good quality aluminium primer for outdoor work. If reusing paint brushes soon wrap in cling film to keep them moist. Put an elastic band round the bristles to keep them together.
When assembling flat packs: read the instructions, which are always impossible, first and have to hand a large mug of sweet tea or whisky for a frayed temper.
Wallpaper: For walls overlap edges by 3mm and work towards a window. The light then shines on the smooth piece at the join which is less visible. For ceilings get Readers Digest DIY manual or refer to YouTube.
Test walls for presence of electric wires before drilling into wall. Make sure that any electric tools are plugged into a RSD source. RSD isolating adapters can be purchased at any good hard ware shop.
Don't use extension leads in heavy rain or across very damp ground. Never rewire an extension lead unless you are a professional. It is too easy to make mistakes.
When rewiring an old plug look carefully at where the old wires went and draw a plan. B<u>r</u>own wires go to the <u>r</u>ight (i.e. live wire to right)
Do not go up tall ladders if on your own.
Measure anything to be cut three times and cut once (tip from a carpenter/builder)
Look for green energy technology tips. Ask a tradesman for advice.
To keep bath water warm and save on energy, remove bath panel, pack the space around the bath with fibreglass and replace the panel. To save heating energy set ambient temperature to max $18°$. This is pleasant rather than too hot and dry.

Carry a mobile phone if working on a roof.
To treat for woodworm: Do not be tempted to spray yourself as the fumes are very toxic.

Decorating and Colour *given by a professional interior design and decorator*

Prepare the room, materials and scheme before starting.
Choose fabrics first if choosing plain walls as it's easier to match paint to fabric than vice versa.
Colour: Paint sample boards at least A3 size so you can move them around the room. Look at them at different times of day as colour varies with light. Stick any wallpaper and fabrics you may want on the colour boards so as to get an overall picture of the scheme. (A Mood Board) A good mood I hope.
The ground work will pay off. Filling, sanding, caulking and mist coats on fresh plaster will make the finished product look better – don't cut corners. Keep brushes and tin with as little paint on/in as possible. Brushes should only have paint one third of way up bristles. Wipe off excess paint from woodwork, over plugs, switches etc. as you go.
Painting is fun but only if you are in control. Make sure floor and furniture protection is in place before starting. Rollered paint splatters everywhere- yes, I mean everywhere. Do the top coat of your woodwork after rollering to avoid a speckled, rough finish. Use lots of cotton rags.
People get muddled with which paint goes where. Walls are usually painted in emulsion-silk finish or matt; woodwork in oil or acrylic eggshell or gloss. Dulux call acrylic eggshell satinwood. Clean tools for acrylic paints and emulsions in water and oil based painting tools with white spirit.
Baby wipes get paint off anything.
Use paint kettles to carry small amounts of paint about.

For any interior design consultancy call Pip Scaramanga on 07970611290 or pipscaramanga7@gmail.com

EDUCATION

Getting adolescent boys to school without a fuss: You can't!
When learning anything, think of it as filling a glass from a jug of water: Go slowly and the glass will fill exactly. Rush and a lot spills over and is wasted.
Given by elderly London cabby and given to him by an elderly instructor.

Exams

Revising: Start early. Make a programme. Take breaks.
Don't listen to music especially if it has words.
Find out your learning style. It may be visual, kinaesthetic (doing and acting things) or oral (listening, reciting, record & listen again). Make a mind map or spider diagram. Put labels around the room. **For English revision**: All the standard tips apply plus your best learning style. For example:
Read and re read the book or choose pages at random and think how they fit in the narrative.
Make a mind map of the book. Write down notes on each character.
Taking exams: Do not panic. Read all the instructions at the top. Read the questions carefully. If there is no time left jot down the main points. In Maths, physics and Chemistry show your workings. **In English** write for as long as the time you have got. Don't just finish, elaborate.
If you have no idea what the answer is, have a go.
A schoolgirl came out of her GCSE history exam and on being asked how she got on replied "Ok, I think. I did the WW1 ones and wrote all about The Archduke in Sarajevo, how Hitler invaded Poland and how he won the war." The friend replied "But he DIDN'T!" Her reply, "Oh but he was doing so well."

Tips for younger children

To learn the names of the Kings and Queens of England, teach them this rhyme:

Willy, Willy, Harry, Steve;
Harry, Dick, John, Harry 3;
One two three Neds, Richard 2;
Henry 4, 5, 6, then who?
Edward 4, 5, Dick the bad;
Harrys twain and Ned the lad;
Mary, Elizabeth, James the vain;
Charlie cum Charlie, James again;
Four Georges, William and Victoria;
Edward, George and then our Queen!

FIELD SPORTS

Fishing *given by a non angler.*
Take a fishing rod.
(Other tips are given by devotees of their particular type of fishing and a Scottish ghillie)
If a beginner, get good instruction. Remember that fishing kills more people than any other sport. Be careful not to let carbon fibre rods touch overhead lines. Ask a local person for information on the river e.g. for best fly to use, good runs or pools and the local rules – which fish may be taken and which put back, obtaining a licence etc. Wear blunt ended scissors on a string around the neck or attached to a fishing waistcoat; also a string around the neck attached to a wading stick to prevent it floating away.

Wet fly fishing – for salmon
The rivers tend to be larger and more dangerous. If a river is large or liable to spate floods and a life jacket is advised, wear it.

Life jacket safety
Look for expiry date on gas cylinder and check by blowing the jacket up via its tube and leave overnight. It's safe if it stays blown up.

A Lady who was fishing on the Royal Dee, looked up and saw the Queen Mother on the bank. She immediately curtseyed and her waders filled up with water. She was lucky only to lose her dignity.

For **salmon fishing** the cast is made slightly downstream and the fly travels on downwards. Salmon anglers tend to call them fish and other fish are given their specific names. Overhead casting is usual for a novice – Spey casting is good when banks are high or wooded. The fly is attached to the main line by a lighter line, the cast. The type of fly and floating or sinking cast depends on the state and temperature of the water.

Use a small fly and floating line in low, warmer water, a large fly and sinking line in high, colder water which is usually in the spring or autumn. Keep fly hooks sharp and check the line for knots. Salmon tend to come up the river after rainfall. Overcast and calm days are ideal.

"You won't catch a fish if you don't have a fly in the water".

Catching one's first fish is always exciting. The editor was given good advice when having her first fish, a boisterous grilse (first year salmon), on the line,

she called to the ghillie on the bank, "I think I'm going to have a heart attack." He replied, "Don't you dare till you get it on the bank!"
Another time, having a foot jammed between rocks, she shouted downstream for help. Her husband called back, rather less helpfully, "Try putting one foot in front of the other".

Dry fly fishing–The dry fly floats on the top of the water and fish have a wide angle of vision - 180° vision - therefore be very careful not to be seen especially when in a clear water chalk stream. Wear dull clothing and never anything white which reflects the light. Stay low. You will need Polaroid glasses to see below the surface of the water, a many pocketed waistcoat, a broad brimmed hat, landing net, bag for spare gear, a "priest" to dispatch fish to be kept and a bag to put it in. Fish swim upstream catching flies as they float downstream. Cast upstream just ahead of the fish without a splash. Let leader float gently onto water.

Fish conservation

Boycott threatened fish, such as tuna, sea bass and salmon netted at sea. It's said that 70% of the world's largest pelagic fish have been lost since the 1970s.

Buy certified sustainable fish with the Marine Stewardship Council logo.
Go to www.msc.org and support them.

Fishing tackle can be obtained at Taunton Angling Centre or any reputable anglers' shop.

Fishing from rocks: Never fish in high seas. It is too dangerous.

Sea fishing from a boat: Watch how you are going to get back to the harbour. Be aware that a strong wind can make you drift quickly. Put out a sea anchor (drogue).
Watch out for strong currents and tides. If old lead pipes are available these make good weights. Weights can be made by making a hole in damp sand as a mould or better still putting a piece of copper tubing into damp sand. Melt a scrap of lead in an old soup can, pour the lead into the mould and insert a wire loop made from a wire coat hanger and allow it to set.

Fishing for sea bass from beach or rocks (these should always be put back as they are a threatened species): Only worry about the water you can cover

with a cast. The rest is immaterial.
Tying flies: Underdressed flies are like underdressed girls, better and more attractive.

Shooting
Keep all kit in the same place. Get ready the night before.
Don't tie your dog to your cartridge bag. Don't use your foot or shooting stick to anchor your dog. You land up with a sore back and considerable loss of dignity. Remember the number of your stand.
Never put different sized cartridges in the same bag. This can lead to fatalities. Before loading make sure barrel is clear. Mud can easily get into it e.g. when climbing a bank.
When climbing a stile or fence: break and unload the gun and if handing it to someone else let them see that the barrels are clear. Don't fire at low birds when the beat is coming to an end.
Don't shoot unless you can see clearly. This is particularly important when shooting up hill.
When a bird is coming along the line follow the routine "bum, belly, beak, fire". When shooting and the sun is bright and low in the sky, close the master eye while waiting for the birds otherwise the master eye changes.

FINANCES

Giving to charity
If undecided on an amount, give the larger one. You are much less likely to regret it.
For retiring collection at funerals the same applies; plus write a cheque giving post code on back and say if tax paid and ask for gift aid to be taken.

Giving to teenagers
Ask parents what is being collected for and give extra. Things are much more expensive than expected.

Energy
Compare quotes and possible fixed price contracts. Consider switching energy supplier as this could save over £200 in energy bills and form or join a local group to buy oil at bulk prices.
Turn off appliances and don't leave on standby. Have hot water timed not constant.
Use thermostats properly. Switch off electric kettle as soon as it starts boiling.

Paying tax *given by a retired tax collector*
Filling in self assessment tax form for first time: Read the whole document and any instructions carefully. If in doubt phone the local office first. Fill in with pencil first.

Insurance
Compare quotes for any insurance whether buying or renewing. Consider paying by monthly direct debit to get a discount.

Investing
When investing money do it on the basis of it not costing anything and no risk of capital loss *(What a Utopia!)*

Finance for mortgages
Compare quotes and fixed rate deals. Take advantage of present low interest rates. Look at interest rates on Store and Credit cards - store cards normally charge high rates. Pay off the debt with the highest interest rate first. Think of switching to Bank loans which normally have lower interest rates than cards. Look on the internet for financial bargains.

Fundraising
When fundraising for large sums of money, appoint a chairman with many contacts who is wealthy enough to donate a large sum of money to the charity him/herself; also a committee prepared to work hard and to organise at least one fundraising event or project themselves. Email committee members 2 months and then 1 month in advance to remind them of the date and time of meetings or events. Be prepared to ask a member who cannot give full commitment to stand down. (*One fundraiser for a project needing several million pounds returned a paltry cheque to a wealthy donor with a tactful but firm letter. The replacement cheque had moved the decimal point twice.)*

GARDENING
given by the Head Gardener of a garden open to the public

Plan the year's work well ahead to avoid repetition.

Garden little and often unless a lot of tools are involved. Take all the tools you are likely to use to the area to be worked on. Schedule tasks for the day so that on hot days you are working in the shade in the afternoon and vice versa.

If you pull up a plant and it comes back it was a weed. If you pull up a plant and it never comes back then it <u>was</u> a plant.

Dismiss as nonsense any suggestion of a labour saving garden. Like children, plants need love and care and who has ever heard of labour saving children? When work gets too arduous, hand over to someone else.

If you **want the garden to look smart** and have limited time, mow the lawn and cut the edges neatly. Do the Chelsea chop – so called because it is carried out in late May/early June, at the time of the Chelsea Flower Show. Cut late flowering perennials such as Sedum, Phlox and Asters by 1/3 to ½. This promotes the growth of side shoots producing more compact, prolific and slightly later flowers. When there are a few plants the front can be cropped, leaving the rear un-cropped. Many plants may be cropped, others not. This giving staggered flowering .

The owner of a larger garden was asked "How many gardeners work in your garden?" She replied, "Mmmm. About half."

To remove weeds from a lawn organically, treat with sulphate of iron in spring or autumn. Rake well with wire rake (scarify) twice yearly. This will set most weeds back including small dandelions. Large dandelions will need to be removed by hand. Moss will persist in a domestic compost bin and is best burnt or put in a municipal wheely bin.

Naming plants: When moving house, if possible, go round the garden with the previous owner and write down the plants' names as a list and write them into a prepared garden plan. For new plants use permanent labels such as Macpenny (you scratch the name on the black tag) or Alitags (aluminium labels), plus for your own use bury a label near the plant (always in a similar spot e.g. on the right (or 3 o'clock).

Losing tools. Tie long coloured string on to garden scissors (or bright ribbon or scarf).

Paint handles of tools with bright enamel paint and surround with a band of bright insulating tape.
Tulip bulbs: feed after flowering and remove all dead heads to stop seed formation. When leaves yellow, lift and dry. Plant them in the spring with bone meal below and water with nitrogen-rich fertilizer (tomato food).
To aid **fertilisation of lone plum** or greengage tree: cut 2 or 3 bunches of blackthorn blossom. Put stalks in plastic bag. Fill with water and secure open end of bag with elastic band and tie to branches of tree.
Sick tree e.g. quince with rust. Water around the base with feed in the spring but if this is a lawn cut the bottom off a large Coke bottle, make a hole through the turf and fill with feed. This avoids a lush lawn. *(It worked for me. I also threatened the tree first with felling if it was not better in 2 years.)*
Bindweed: For long stems employ a long stick, bunch up the stems then spray them. Baby bindweed: cut bottom off small fruit juice bottle. Screw it down over the shoots and spray them through the neck.
A gardener does as much harm as a slug of equal size.
Sow radish with lettuce or spinach, harvest them when ready and thin the main crop at same time.
To prevent rabbits from eating roses, put several sticks (e g kindling) in a pot and fill with Jeyes fluid. Leave till thoroughly damp then put near roses.
To stop badgers, use strong Jeyes fluid solution to water across their entry tracks.
To grow a **camomile lawn**: take a fresh bag of camomile tea and scatter the myriads of seeds.
For a flower lawn, sew yellow rattle seeds first which will weaken the coarse grasses and allow other finer grass and flower species to grow.
Stake **delphiniums** in the winter and in the spring. Put a sprinkling of wood ash and soot around them to deter slugs. Sand will also deter slugs. Put a very few pellets of slug bait away from the plant and under a stone. Putting slug bait on the plants only attracts the slugs to the plant.
Cuttings: either buy prepared mixture for cuttings or make up mixture with 50% sterilized compost (all commercial compost is sterilised) and 50% sharp sand. This can be bought or use sharp river sand. Never use sea sand or builders' sand which will kill the cuttings or simply put them into water and watch them grow roots.
Homemade compost is not safe as it may contain diseases such as fungi.

Making homemade compost: Keep hot and a little damp. Add activator such as Garotta or urine. In large gardens build 3 brick bins and cover with old carpet. If using food which is ideal for compost beware of rats which carry the dangerous Weill's disease. Put good rat poison in a length of drain and cover with carpet. Alternatively call the rat catcher (rodent officer in modern parlance). When living in a remote country area I once called the rodent officer who arrived in smart clothes and car but pronounced that he could not do anything as these were country rats and he only knew about town rats.

Protect pea seeds and yellow crocuses from mice: Put chopped up gorse above seeds or corms and cover with soil.

Plant a sweet scented plant like daphne odorata, winter sweet or sarcococcus near a frequently used path e.g. leading to the front door.

If **moving to a new area** see what grows in your area and find out the nature of the soil. Like what you grow don't grow what you like.

When choosing a rose think about length and frequency of flowering. Be careful of size and height. If possible choose a scented variety.

(I was once at the Chelsea Flower Show in the late afternoon and remarked to a helper at the stand of a well known rose nursery that a supposedly scented rose didn't seem to smell. She replied "Ah well, it has run out of scent. It has been sniffed at too often today.")

To separate young plants that are too tightly packed together in their pot, float them in a bucket of water and gradually separate the roots. Lower each one into its prepared hole and fill in gently with compost.

To prevent **cabbage white butterflies** from laying eggs on vegetables use Enviromesh (butterfly/bird netting), available at Monkton Elm, Taunton; Kelways, Langport; or any good garden centre.

To prevent carrot fly damage, put an 8" shield around the plants or sow in a raised bed. The carrot fly can only fly over a 6" shield.

To grow runner beans against a sunny wall, run a wire across the top and then drop strings from it and attach them to a thick stick or better a cable with 2" rings laid on the ground.

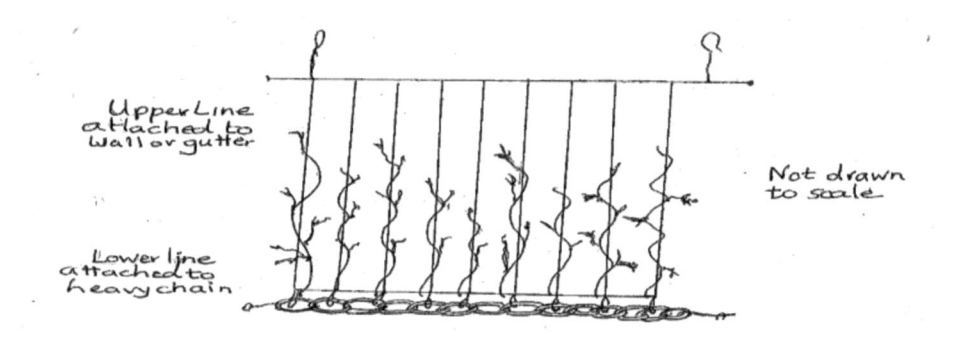

[Diagram: Upper Line attached to wall or gutter; Lower line attached to heavy chain. Not drawn to scale.]

Revitalise soggy swell gel by leaving in the hot cupboard for a week.
Tomatoes – Use inverted plastic flower pots with the base removed, instead of culture rings. Feed through pot and water at base.
Care of tools: Lock all access doors. Clean well before stowing. Hang tools on a board or wall in their appointed place with the outline of the tool handle painted on the board or wall. Always use the same position and check that all tools are away before leaving the garden shed. Keep secateurs and loppers clean and dry. Oil occasionally with WD40. Sharpen when required with small sharpener (such as Lansky Blade Medic sharpener).
Save water by having rain water butts under suitable roof drains and use the water for watering. Using a watering can is much more economical than using a hose. If your plants need a lot of water think of getting more plants that thrive in a hot and dry climate including many silver leaved plants.
Slug control: Encourage birds especially thrushes and blackbirds by having bird feed available. Use slug pellets sparingly under a cloche or stone some distance from the threatened plant. Surround the plant with sharp sand or soot. If in a pot, stick a copper band or (cheaper) a thick band of engine grease, obtainable at a garage, around it. Put empty orange or grapefruit skin upside down and collect slugs the next day or go out at night with a torch and throw the slugs into a bucket of salty water. For **hostas** water with a nematode which infects and kills slugs.
Cleaning green slippery **flagstones**: Treat with Jeyes Fluid.
Treating a plant for **honey fungus**: Jeyes Fluid can be used instead of Armillotox which is expensive. Trees that have died of honey fungus need to be taken out with as much of the root system as possible. Try to site any new plant away from the infected area and choose a plant that is less prone to

infection. If the garden is small and you are willing to risk planting a new tree in the same area, dig a large hole where the dead tree was, taking out any old roots and burning them, treat the walls of the hole with Jeyes Fluid and import new soil from elsewhere.

Old rose beds: Roses will finally exhaust the soil they are in. They may need to be thrown out. If very precious try pruning, root pruning and moving to another site. If a rose has to go into an old existing bed, dig a hole a bit larger than normal, put a large cardboard box into the hole and plant the rose in the box in imported soil or compost.

Aphids: Stop using systemic insecticides which kill all the natural predators such as ladybirds and get a lacewing box for lacewings to occupy in the winter. Clean aphids off with foamy washing up detergent. White fly in greenhouse: Attract them to yellow card (such as the cover of Yellow Pages) covered in thick car grease. Use an imported nematode. Reporting the invasive harlequin ladybirds is not obligatory but information can be found on the internet about them.

To **propagate primroses** you need a mixture of the two types of Primrose. On looking carefully at the centre top of the flower you see the pin-eyed variety which has a tiny greenish disc on a long stem. When the flower is pulled apart the pollen can be seen below the disc. In the thrum-eyed variety you see the golden pollen and the pin is well below it. Hence the bee can carry the pollen between the two varieties.

Get a bench and sit on it.

Waste not, Want not

Sow seeds in cores of loo roll filed with compost.
Rattan blinds make good windshields. Use the bottom one third of milk containers with holes cut in the bottom as flower pots. They are useful when travelling with seedling gifts.
Baskets from chest freezers make good plant protectors.

Save wire spirals from notebooks and calendars to fix a plant to a pole. Stretch out the coil and fix first to the pole staking at the top and then round the plant.
Use old CD's hung loosely on string as bird scarers.
Make your own labels out of plastic milk containers.

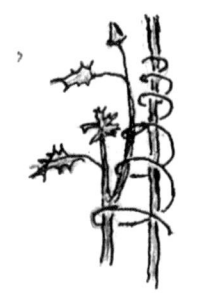

Put corks or small plastic pots on tops of sticks to prevent injuries or to support a net.
Use a Coke bottle with the bottom cut off and no lid as a mini greenhouse but beware, it can overheat and kill the plant.
Hang banana skins in the greenhouse to hasten ripening of tomatoes.
Broken up tea bags provide good acid mulch for azaleas in pots.
Wrap bubble wrap round large pots and fleece over top to prevent frost damage.
For small gardens and **arthritic hands** used 10 litre emulsion buckets to make good, light buckets.
For fine weeding wear a pair of latex gloves
A DIY tool for removing tacks makes a good mini trowel for weeds in pots.

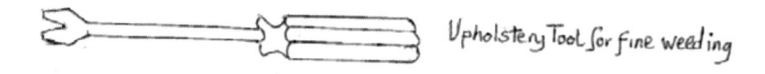

Upholstery Tool for fine weeding

Use an old shower door unit on its hinges as a cover for a cold frame

Helping nature in your garden: *given by a former Deputy Chairman of the CNCC for Northern Ireland*

Don't be too tidy and don't strim - it kills far too many hedgehogs and frogs, all of which keep pests down.
To make a **wild flower lawn**: never fertilise the lawn. Sow yellow rattle seeds first which will weaken the coarse grasses by competing with nutrients and allow finer grass and wild flowers to grow. Only mow the lawn in early spring or late autumn/winter. Recruit woofers *(workers on organic farms - a European wide organisation)* to mow in the late autumn and take the grass and flowers to make wildflower hay. Gather wild flower seeds from your locality and spread them on your area. Don't use packets of wild flowers as they contain foreign seeds. The older the lawn gets the poorer the soil and the richer the flowers.

Houseplants

Most houseplants like to be watered from below. Hyacinths: water initially, then put in dark place and do not water till really dry. When green shoot comes up put them in the light and water well.

Weather
If a lot of mole hills appear at the same time then 4 days dry weather lies ahead. *(Told by a farmer but not authenticated.)*

How to help at a Chelsea Flower Show Stand
Have stamina. Know the owner's plants. Be good at mental arithmetic.

How to be a good Garden Designer
Get to know the neighbourhood. Note what plants grow locally, soil conditions and prevailing wind. Find out your client's vision. If they don't have one, teach them how to. Ultimately you must provide them with a garden that they will love. Discuss how much help will be needed for maintenance. Make a plan (even a rough one on an envelope will do.). Establish the garden framework with trees and hedges and any hard landscaping. Trees should frame distant vistas and balance with the architecture of the house. Hedges will outline the garden space and also provide inner divisions, providing a background to further planting. Choose the smaller shrubs, perennials and bulbs to give the garden colour and interest through all the seasons. Do not overlook late-summer performers. Listen to how your client will use the garden. Discourage him/her from labour-intensive schemes which can be added later. Discourage wild flower meadows initially. They are difficult and expensive.

How to be a good Landscape Designer
Know your plants (trees, shrubs and flowers) as well as working as an apprentice or volunteer in a good garden or botanical garden. Doing a course is the icing on the cake.

HEALTH AND FIRST AID

Health

(For carbon monoxide poisoning and diarrhoea and vomiting – see kitchen safety.)

General well-being. When very nervous (e.g. before an exam) or you have had enough use Dr. Bach's Rescue Remedy – four drops on the tongue.

An Irish pick-me-up useful after any cold sport: 1/2 sherry and 1/2 ginger wine (not ale).

Walk for 20 mins each day if possible. Always walk to a pub on the top of a hill.

Make sure that you know what the drugs you are taking are for. If you are on a lot and feeling generally unwell ask your Doctor if they could be interfering with each other.

Washing hands with antiseptic soap is no better than ordinary soap. It is the method, such as washing between the fingers and the duration that matters. *(In the 60's there was a bad outbreak of diarrhoea in a military camp. The outbreak was only stopped when 2 armed soldiers were placed outside the latrine and made sure that all personnel washed their hands properly for 3 minutes.)*

When to take a sick baby to the doctor: Consult the book "Baby Check" by Paediatric Professor Colin Morley. It works on a point system for each cause for anxiety. The higher the points the more urgent the case e.g. floppy drowsiness carries a very high score; green vomit and blood on nappy are high but not as high as the drowsiness. The ISBN is 9780955969102.

To stop a baby crying if not hungry or thirsty, rock the baby in your arms at the same time as bending your knees up and down. Put the baby near a dishwasher or washing machine. The sound is similar to that in the womb. Take him/her to an all night supermarket. Play some soothing music or sing a lullaby.

"If I had known then what I know now I would have kept my legs in a jar."

If your drugs have changed colour or do not seem to be working inform doctor who will notify correct authority. It has recently been introduced that patients as well as doctors can report these changes. Soon after this change came in a man with schizophrenia reported that someone was interfering with his antidepressant pills and had changed their colour and made them ineffective. A panel naturally thought this was a symptom of his paranoia but one member disagreed and said they should follow the rules. Investigation showed that the drugs were a fraudulent import from the Far East.

To abort a cold at sore throat stage: take 2 chewable 20 gm vitamin C pills. Gargle with diluted TCP. Have a hot drink of honey, lemon juice and a clove.

To prevent hay fever: Rub some Vaseline round the inside of the nose as high as possible. (*It worked for the tip donor.*)

Diarrhoea: Flat Coke will give you the necessary electrolytes and sugar (NOT Diet Coke). Diarrhoea abroad – use coconut milk instead.

Constipation: Rub tummy gently with the flat of your hand, round and round, moving in a clockwise direction i.e. up the right side, across the top and down the left side. (This is the direction taken by the large bowel.)

Colic: Try any antacid in liquid or tablet form that contains an aluminium derivative. If severe and persistent consult a doctor.

Cramp: This is caused by a build up of lactic acid in muscle. Try to stretch and massage the muscle. Immerse the cramped area in hot water to improve the blood supply. Dip a finger into salt and lick it. Take a heaped teaspoonful of sodium bicarbonate in a little water (Sodium bicarbonate can also be obtained in capsules). If cramps are persistent consult your Doctor.

To prevent cramps in bed keep a medium sized potato in the bed. (The donor swore by this and travelled with her potato – perhaps it keeps the legs moving!). Quinine (and therefore tonic water) helps to prevent cramp.

For itchy skin in the elderly: After having tried changing washing powder (stop biological powder) get cream or balm and rub in after bath. Add Cetraben emollient to the bathwater for 6 weeks.

Foot care *given by a podiatric surgeon*

Don't try any heroic surgery on your own feet. Seek professional objective opinion – your subjective opinion may be wrong. For rough skin on soles a file with the head at an angle (available from Boots) is useful. Use emulsifying cream to soften skin. A suitably shaped piece of cotton wool can be placed between adjacent toes that are rubbing into each other.

First Aid

Wasp stings: Apply anything alkaline e.g. baking soda and antihistamines (sting relief).

Bee stings: Apply vinegar. Leave the sting in and use sting relief.

Burns: Hold under cold tap immediately then use antihistamine or a paste of sodium bicarbonate and water (not for caustic acid burns).
When in a remote area, if wounded, fresh urine is a good supply of sterile cleansing liquid.
Never be tempted however thirsty to drink urine (or sea water). They make matters worse.
Treading on a sea-urchin: The extreme pain is due to the alkalinity. Steep in urine which is acidic, as is vinegar.
Sudden loss of vision in one eye (not following an accident): Rub vigorously (it may move a minute clot on), then follow this up with your Doctor. Rubbing an eye that has been hit can be dangerous as the loss of vision may be due to a detached retina.
For a **foreign body in the eye** ask someone to lick it out if it's not easily visible. The tongue is soft and can go under the upper lid. If it is visible, remove with corner of hanky. Any dangerous fluid in eye: wash copiously with water under a running tap with lids held open then consult your doctor.
Attend a resuscitation demonstration for **person collapsed** in street or house.
Bruise under nail: This can be extremely painful and is best treated by a doctor or nurse. If not available, heat a strong sharp needle in a hot flame and drive it through the nail to release trapped blood.

How to relax

Lie down on your side. Hold your arm up high and bring it down very slowly until it reaches nearly all the way then let it flop down. Relax all your body muscles, limbs and face. Let any external sounds drift through your mind, be aware of them. Stay like that for 5-10 mins.
Lie down and totally relax. Breathe deeply in and out counting 1, 2, 3 in and 2, 2, 3 out with each breath. Think of a beautiful place, go on breathing and counting then just be in that place.
Meditation is similar to relaxing (above) type 2 but better done sitting up, eyes closed; a mantra is used (a soothing word) which is constantly and slowly repeated. A dream-like state is achieved. After a few minutes, or longer, give a shake and come back into the world about you.

Coping with cancer

Live for each day rather than worrying about the future.

For nausea while on chemo- or radiotherapy: Drink plenty of water and try avocados on toast or in a sandwich or anything you fancy, as in pregnancy. Try a visualization technique: Use the total relaxation technique given in (2) above and, while deeply relaxed and in a beautiful place, visualize your defensive white blood corpuscles engulfing and then gobbling up the cancer cells. Concentrate on this task for about 10 minutes.

Defensive white cells destroying cancer cell

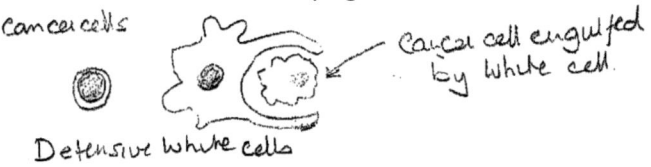

[Hand-drawn diagram: Cancer cells on the left, with a defensive white cell shown engulfing a cancer cell. Labels: "Cancer cells", "Cancer cell engulfed by white cell", "Defensive white cells"]

How to get to sleep
There are four methods. Use the method for relaxing above then stay in a drowsy state.
Read a boring book. Use the classic counting sheep method. Keep repeating the word for a favourite food or object such as "whisky" or "beach".

How to get back to sleep
Try method above. Listen to the World Service. Abandon trying and get up, have a cup of tea and pick up brownie points by doing extra tasks. Melatonin is now available on prescription (it is very expensive) and may regularise the sleep pattern.

Slimming
Join a club such as Weight Watchers. Avoid sugary drinks including sweetened fruit juice, fatty foods and carbohydrates especially when these two are mixed, but have a balanced diet. (See beautician.) When helping yourself, take half the amount that you would have liked or, if the plate is already full, put half of it back or to one side.
When finishing off children's irresistible leftovers -don't; or count it as part of your next meal.
When hungry, have a drink instead of something to eat or just clean your teeth.

It is a deplorable fact but true, that there were no fat people in Nazi held prison camps. The editor, as a newly fledged junior doctor found a lady weeping in a side ward. She had a difficult condition which causes, not only infertility, but also intractable obesity. In reply to, "Oh dear, what is the matter?" She said, "Oh Doctor, someone opened the door and my lunch blew away."

Disability

Talking to deaf people: Don't shout and don't assume that they are imbeciles. Let them see your lips.

Helping blind people: Ask if they would like help and if yes, "How?". Let him/her take your arm and follow you. If you take their arm you will end up pushing them. Help them to join the RNIB. Offer to read to them or get talking books from the Library.

The blind can now obtain an app to send an image of objects such as tinned food or a locality(such as a building) which is then viewed and reported on by a volunteer who will explain the nature of the food or the whereabouts of the door to the building. Apply to be a volunteer through RNIB.

Helping a wheelchair user: In order to find out if help is needed, go to the front of the chair and address the person in the chair not their assistant. This is particularly important for children when it is tempting to speak to the adult and overlook the child. One wheelchair user quoted an occasion when a would-be helper came from behind and, the assistant being absent, wheeled the chair without enquiry in the wrong direction. He also quoted times when, being abroad, he had been treated as an imbecile. When in a crowded area, sit beside the wheelchair user as you will be audible and on an equal footing.

Disability parking: A blue badge holder may park free of charge in any slot with the wheelchair sign on tarmac. They may also park free of charge in any area (on street parking or car park) where there is a local authority blue sign at the pay box or on a nearby post or wall to confirm this rule. This may vary between towns so check with the enforcement office (not just the issuing office) before taking the risk. The rule does _not_ apply to an area not controlled by a local authority.

Speech: Helping someone with a stammer. This is difficult as individuals vary. Interrupting them and providing the missing word may make things worse. For a child with a stammer get help early. There are speech therapists specially trained to help with stammer.

Helping someone who cannot make labial sounds: (i.e. when the tongue comes between the teeth onto the lips such as in "<u>th</u>ink".) They may be subconsciously afraid of being seen putting the tongue out that far. Get them to hold their hand vertically in front of their mouth and try to touch their hand with their tongue. They are able to do it because the fear of being seen has been removed.

Epilepsy: If someone has a grand mal attack (falls to the ground jerking) make sure that they can breathe (i.e. that they are not swallowing the tongue). Lay them on their side, pull the chin up and reassure them that they are OK.

For a relative or friend who has severe sudden attacks, falls down and injures head, make a protective cap. Buy a fashionable black ski cap and provide a cushion for crown. Cut a disk of 1½" thick foam rubber of suitable size for crown and stitch in place. Cover with a layer of ½" felt (this cannot be stitched). Cover all with a cotton lining to keep all in place and stitch. Use a black elastic band under chin to secure. Bicycle helmets are not suitable. They are too large and heavy and invite unwelcome questions.

Ready made up caps can be obtained from http://.tm-leconfortmedical/contact-form,php which gives phone no. and address (They speak good English).

Helping a schizophrenic: *given by a schizophrenia sufferer who was first aware of difficulty when crossing the Sahara and finding an enormous scorpion in his tent.*

Be aware of the difference between "psychosis" and "psychotic". Schizophrenia is a psychosis and the sufferer will hear voices, hallucinate, be unable to put his thoughts or life together and needs sympathy. A psychotic has a dangerous personality disorder and needs to be in a secure psychiatric hospital or, less preferable, in the secure psychiatric unit of a prison.

How to Cope with Old Age *(see also health)*

Learn to lose control – Let the younger generation take over.
If living alone have phone within reach of bath.
Write dates of family and friends' birthdays in diary and reminder 1 week in advance to get a card.

Learn your partner's skills e.g. cooking, home accounts, car savvy, etc.
Make a living will or lasting power of attorney for health and general affairs and inform next of kin and Doctor.
To keep mind active and maintain memory: Play memory games, enjoy friendships, socialise, join a Club or work for a charity, and learn a new skill such as a language. Take regular exercise: 20 mins per day. Put the kettle on for morning tea then walk up and down stairs while it boils. Keep a pet.
Go to bed early. If sleep is missed at night have a rest in the day.
If you are considering a retirement home for yourself, visit it well in advance. Look up in house activities and outings. See what is happening in the day rooms and view their notice boards. If you can afford a private home but are worried about the cost be aware that 24 hour resident care at home may be cheaper.

How to drive safely when growing old
Arrange with a trusted friend/family member to tell you when you need to stop. Then you can drive with more confidence – until? But search for Route 60+ as, though you have survived and kept your licence for decades you can sign up for a full hour with an advanced driving instructor – not a test, just a gentle pointing out of bad habits and reassurance.

Safety in the bath
Have a phone or pendant or wrist alarm (piper alarm in Somerset) near the bath. Wear your piper alarm (or equivalent) at all times especially when in bed. Many falls occur at night when going to the bathroom. Use a rubber mat to prevent slipping. Good long mats made by Home Hardware distributors can be obtained from Boiler Tec in Langport and other good hardware stores, or Croydex mats from David Marsh in Castle Cary. Drain the mat regularly to prevent mould gathering.

Self Protection
If living alone, have a telephone within reach of the bath. On a street, walk on the side facing oncoming traffic and do not wear dangerously provocative clothing. If accosted, shout the name of a fictitious male friend as loud as possible, carry some money and a back-up mobile in a separate pocket. Give

your bag up. In a dubious area carry a rape alarm. Have keys ready to open front door immediately.
Offensive weapons are not allowed but carry your keys separated between your fingers. These can be punched at eyes of assailant.
If abducted drop something distinctive i.e. a wallet or keys, as soon as possible.
If kidnapped: switch off mobile immediately. If you hear of a kidnapping incident don't phone to see if someone is safe. This could reveal their whereabouts and lead to their death. This happened in Nigeria when a number of westerners were killed by Boko Haram.
Do not antagonise your captors – obey their instructions.

How to look after a person with dementia in your home

Consult your local Alzheimer Society (available for any form of dementia). Is there a lunch club that they can go to? Lunch clubs may have singing, puzzles, pottery etc. Can they get to a music/singing group? If possible keep a pet.
Sing their familiar songs or nursery rhymes. Get a CD of familiar music. Talk about their childhood memories, but be careful some people find it distressing if they cannot remember the past. Look at old family photos with them.
Join the Alzheimer's Society (telephone number 02074233500). It helps all dementia sufferers. Persuade your local town to be 'dementia friendly'.
Shops can help by signing up to the dementia friendly society which will help, for instance, when sufferers are lost or overloaded or shop lifting.
Live in the moment. Share jokes while he/she can. Play their favourite music. Don't argue with them, try to divert the subject e.g. "why is my lunch late?" Do not respond with "You have had it already!" but "It's coming soon" or "Which sort of pudding do you like best?"
Talk about memories but be careful as some people find it upsetting that they cannot remember the past anymore.
Play along with their delusion e.g. he/she says "Those men outside are breaking into the car. I must go and get rid of them." Do not say, even said kindly, "Of course they are not, you silly old thing!" but "Oh dear, so they are. I will go and get rid of them straight away." and on coming in say "it's all right now, dear, they have all gone away."

Dementia with aggression and violence is particularly difficult. If you are considering a care home look into all the options and visit the ones you like the sound of. Look at the day rooms as well as the bedrooms and see if there is any noxious smells of incontinence. Do they have a pet? What activities are available? Do they have any music/singing sessions?

A couple with Alzheimer's came to their daughter's door one night, dressed in full rig for a royal garden party, having seen a report of the parties on the TV.

How to help someone who has lost their speech following a stroke

Strokes are very frightening - give lots of sympathy and support. Get a speech therapist to help as soon as possible. Providing the missing word or pointing to letters to spell a word may help. Keep on being sympathetic and helpful and cheerful despite setbacks. Get a pocket sized photo album and make lists of necessary words to slip in the pockets, such as: family and friends' names; parts of house, garden or town; furniture or clothes; food and shopping requirements.

Memory Aids

Cheque stubs: If you often forget to fill these in, put a small coloured removable sticker onto the top blank cheque near where you fill in the amount. When the cheque is filled in and the stub completed, transfer the sticker to the next cheque.

Switching off lights: The editor's elderly and forgetful father used regularly to leave the downstairs loo light on until he took to wearing a cap in the loo. He would remove it as he left and it would remind him to turn off the light.

HOBBIES

Batik *given by a Batik maker and exhibitor*
Batik is a traditional Javanese cotton or silk fabric used for clothing, scarves or wall hangings.
Draw a design on the cloth first. Use a Tjanting with a bamboo handle, copper reservoir and spout to hold the liquid wax and apply to the cloth.
After waxing dye the cloth in vegetable or chemical dye, wash, dry and repeat the wax process in different areas using different dyes in each cycle. Boil the cloth to remove wax – or iron between sheets of newspaper then dry.

Bees and beekeeping

Bees are mostly defensive, not aggressive, so if bees are buzzing around you **don't wave your arms or try to swat them.** Walk quietly back the way you have come if possible through bushes or low trees. If a swarm of bees enter your garden **stay calm**. They are looking for a new home and if left alone will eventually depart. **Keep inquisitive children away** and contact a local beekeeper (see below) who may come and collect them.
If bees have set up a home in or near your home and are not a nuisance leave them alone, otherwise **contact a local beekeeper** or if that is impossible try the Council's Pest Control Service. If a bee is caught in your hair shake your head to dislodge it. **Do not** push your hands through your hair or you will get stung. To find a local beekeeper go to the British Beekeepers' Association website: www.bbka.org.uk or a local website e.g.
www.somersetbeekeepers.org.uk
To take up beekeeping contact your local association who will arrange your training. It is fun and you will be doing your bit for the planet but you do need to know what you are doing. Between 2010 and 2014 there has been a 40% loss of commercial honeybee colonies.
Over 100 of our foodstuffs are dependent on bees. It is said that the number of beekeepers has gone down by 70% since the 1960's**.**

Bird watching

Beginners:
Get good binoculars, 80 x 30 or 10 x 40. Test in shop or try a friend's. A proper harness for binoculars is more comfortable. Clean lenses with spectacle cleaning cloth or silk hanky.
If raining put lens caps on or keep under jacket until needed.
Go with an expert or in a group. If in a group don't chatter. Wear appropriate dull clothing or wear a non-rustling anorak. If in open country, scan through 360°. Always scan with naked eyes before using binoculars.
Buy a good book. Collins Birds is excellent though rather too large for beginners. Jizz is also a good book.

Advanced:
Get a good steady telescope. A tripod is steady in the wind. An elasticated sling is comfortable.
Twitchers: consult the birdline. For Somerset Ornithological Society consult the website www.somersetbirds.net. In other regions use the appropriate website. RSPB Headquarters in Sandy: www.rspb.org.uk. For the spectacular starling flocks in Somerset phone the starling hotline 07866 554142.
Don't trample on crops or gardens.
Improving knowledge of birdsong: Get the book and CD "Collins Guide to Birdsong and Calls of Birds in Britain and Northern Europe". Get an app for birdsong on an android phone. This will listen to the bird you can hear and will identify it.

Bird watching abroad:
Get a book appropriate to destination and study if before leaving. Use a local guide and keep up with him/her. Let local children look through your telescope. They will be amazed. If the child is then noticed to have sticky red eyes, clean lenses thoroughly with wet wipes or better still, medicated hand wipes.

Bird tables:
Get a good one which has a variety of hooks for different nuts and seeds. Goldfinches love niger seeds; long-tailed tits and woodpeckers go for fat balls. A dish for water helps them. Some birds prefer seeds on the ground. If you are away get someone else to feed the birds. Don't give breadcrumbs in the spring. They are bad for chicks. If a species suddenly declines consult

RSPB. The table may need sterilising. Report any dead or stray caged birds to RSPB.

Bridge *given by a professional Bridge teacher*
For beginners: Go for lessons with friends. Remember that there are many ladies (oops people) walking the streets because they failed to take out trumps. Remember that you have a partner. Play or take a course on the internet.
Intermediate players "Bridge Wisdom"
The <u>worst</u> bid of Bridge wisdom is "Lead top of partner's suit". <u>Yes</u> if you have an Ace and the opposition are in a suit contract rather than No Trumps. <u>Yes</u> if you have a doubleton. <u>Yes</u> if you have a run in the suit and the top one is an honour. But: Lead low if you have an honour at the top. Lead the middle one with no honours and play higher next time to avoid looking like a doubleton.
The Real Bridge Gurus:
Ron Klinger on the subject of "<u>Always</u> lead top of partner's suit" – "No, no, a thousand times NO!"
Andrew Robson on the subject of "<u>Always</u> lead top of partner's suit" said "This method has the merit of simplicity, but has proved too costly. Best is simply to lead the normal card if partner has not bid the suit."

Flower Arranging
Cut stems diagonally then immerse stem tips in boiling water for 3 seconds.
Tulips: pierce stem with pin just below bloom to stay upright. Another method is to put something copper in the water – a 2p coin works.
Hellebores: cut stems very short and float in a bowl. They last much longer.
Mahonia: Either use individual sprays or take whole heads, plunge the stem in boiling water and then put into oasis or spiked wire device in shallow bowl.
When doing a **large arrangement**, keep scissors on a long string around neck. To remove gold lily pollen from clothes or furnishings act at once. Remove with hand held vacuum cleaner or with sellotape wound round hand.
Beware of commercial sachets for prolonging life they may cause bloom on glass vase (strongly suspected but cannot be proven). For any arrangement in water, a soluble aspirin will prolong the life.

To revive floppy cyclamen: lay diagonally on 3 sheets newspaper, then roll up, plunge in narrow bucket filled with water. Leave overnight. To revive floppy roses cut stems diagonally then float in water for approx 3-4 hours. Forsythia can be cut when in bud and will open well in the warm.
Cut holly with berries well before Christmas. Put in a bucket of damp sand and keep outside covered with a net to guard against birds.

Old Cars *given by an Alvis owner since 1988*

Old cars are expensive dreams. Decide what the car is for – racing, rallying, and intercontinental touring, showing ("pot collecting"), club events or just going to the pub.

Having decided the Marque, Model and Year which best meets your hopes buy the car in the best condition you can afford. This will be the cheapest in the long term, unless you are capable of carrying out much restoration work on the mechanics, bodywork and electrics.

Never buy used tyres or parts for brakes or steering, unless vetted by an expert. Your life and those of others depend on this.

(The ignorant editor's schoolgirl Pocket Oxford Dictionary (1932) gave marque as a licence to take enemy ships but her Collins English Dictionary 1979 gives, more logically, an emblem or name plate used to identify a product especially a car. From the French "marquer" – to mark.)

Painting *given by a long term amateur watercolourist*

For beginners Join a class and get advice including on types of paint, brushes and paper to use. Remember "KISS" – Keep It Simple Stupid.

Intermediate amateurs. *Given by a professional artist and teacher.* If you want perfection, give up painting and stick pins in butterflies instead.

The trick is not to get what is "out there" onto your piece of paper – it is to make people think that what is on your piece of paper is "out there".

No matter how fast you work, the light moves faster. Stick with your original vision or chase after shadows. It's up to you. Trees are difficult – Constable spent a lot of time painting broccoli.

Whether it's a lake, a mountain, a forest, or a valley, you are actually painting the weather. An inspiring landscape doesn't make an inspiring painting: that is the job of your mind.

You can't paint everything, you can only edit.

Try to get to the point where you don't know where you are going. You may end up where you started, but at least the journey will have been interesting. Experiment at every opportunity, but remember that when you invite the unexpected you must expect the uninvited.

Singing
Sing with your whole body right down to the pelvic floor. (That is why you can't sing properly when you need a pee). Do warm up exercises. Get lessons and/or join a choir.
If in a choir attend regularly and arrive on time. Don't chatter except during interval or before and after rehearsal. Practise at home. Get a choral CD of work. Sing in front of a mirror. Some people tend to turn head sideways which needs correcting. When performing, watch the conductor. Sing each piece as if it is your favourite – give it your all. Don't sway when performing. Retire before you have to.

Walking
There is no such thing as bad weather only inappropriate clothing. In case of thunder storm: Fork lightning is more dangerous than sheet lightning. Judge the distance of a storm by counting the time between lightning and thunder (approx 1 sec/mile). Stand under a tall tree abandoning metal sticks, umbrellas or caps with metal badge. Gum boots are safer than shoes. A car is safe provided no piece of metal or car sickness protection device is trailing on the ground.
Be aware of tick area for Lyme disease. Don't pull tick off. Kill with surgical spirit or gin.
When gathering wild mushrooms discard any with white gills. If one has been put with true field mushrooms discard them all and wash hands thoroughly – they are deadly.
Walking in a remote area. Clean dirty wounds with urine if no clean water is available. It is initially sterile. Lichen grows on the north side of trees. There are more and thicker branches on the south side of trees.
Preventing leech bites – smother skin with soap. Don't attempt detaching them. Hit with hard blow and they will drop off.

Napoleonic March. When very tired, run 30 paces then walk 30 paces. Not generally recognised so try at own risk!

Mountain Walking
Use Ordnance Survey maps to plan walk – they can be downloaded to a mobile phone or navigation device. Wear good quality boots and clothes. It is worth the expense.
Pack high energy snacks, water, a warm layer and rainwear. Use a compass. Carry a mobile phone with contact and emergency service numbers. Tell someone where you are going and when you expect to return.

Learning a new language
Choose a good teacher. Practise 10 minutes each day. Listen to tapes or CDs in the car. Try a Linguaphone or BBC course.

Silversmithing
If embarking on this hobby, a few days course is not adequate. The goldsmiths have instituted proper courses. There are short ones for beginners and longer ones for those who have done the introductory courses. They are held in London and around England (see their websites).

Learning to play a musical instrument *given by a former tutor at the Junior Department of the Royal College of Music*
Learning to read music is tricky. Once you understand clefs and bar lines find some sheet music of tunes you love (charity shops are a good source). Avoid the ones with complicated sharps and try to decipher them. Try the melody lines first. It is satisfying to recognise themes and melodies as they appear and your sight reading will improve rapidly.

HOSPITALITY

Being a good guest

Arrive and leave when you say you are going to. It is especially important if leaving after breakfast as delays may cause your host to miss appointments. Advice to children going as guest: Get up, eat up and clear up (e.g. offer to clear table or to dry up but putting things away in the wrong place can be counterproductive).

If taking a gift of food: take considerably more than you would eat yourself. Let host know in advance of any dietary preferences or allergies e.g. nuts, shell/sea food, gluten, etc. For **gluten free** warn your hosts well in advance that cornflour instead of wheat flour is needed. Take own rice biscuits.

Vegetarian: offer to eat only vegetables. Take own apples to save embarrassment. **Diabetic**: warn in advance and take own supply of sweet food or glucose in case meal is delayed. If taking flowers: cut flowers may be an embarrassment as host may already have made his/her own arrangements and may still be preparing food. A plant in a pot might be better or cut flowers that are already arranged. The stems can be put in a plastic bag secured with an elastic band and water added.

Overnight loo etiquette: Ask if flushing will awaken others. Some plumbing can be very noisy and the sound travels along the pipes. Dry feet before stepping onto a communal bathmat. When leaving, ask your host what is to be done with the bed. If told that a "daily" will do it leave appropriate tip.

To stay awake at a boring dinner party put your little finger between your teeth. You will bite it as you nod off. Answer invitations as soon as possible. If you have a former engagement always stick to it except in the case of bereavement or unforeseen important family need. A lady once failed to respond to an embassy invitation to a Royal occasion. She arrived at the function (which occurred 3 months later) and said to the official greeting guests, "I'm sorry I didn't reply to the invitation." To which the reply was "That's all right madam. It was our fault for inviting you."

When to say thank you for a party/dinner/lunch: Phone first day after event. Write two days after. Send flowers 3 days after. Over a month: abject apology and flowers. You may never be asked again and may lose a friend – but "a lady never takes offence".

Being a good host *Given by the owners of two small and excellent hotels in Langport*

First impressions are vital: there is no second chance to have a go at renewing them.

Cleanliness and quality are essential. Treat people as if they are your friends. Make sure that you are certain of your guests' names before making any introductions. Offer them some refreshment as soon as they are comfortably seated. Introduce them to each other. If there are two or more of you acting as host make sure, if possible, that at least one of you is with them at any time.

Ask well in advance if there are any aversions, allergies or dietary needs. Establish in advance the time of arrival and leaving. This can save a lot of embarrassment later. If you make a full breakfast just leave a selection of goodies out for them to help themselves. Put flowers in the bedroom and have beds well aired and room(s) warm. Leave the wherewithal to make tea in the room plus water, glasses and a tin of biscuits in the room. Lotus caramelised biscuits are delicious for this. Leave water glasses in bathroom. Check bedside lights work in advance and leave one on near their arrival time.

Establish, before retiring, bathing and hot water arrangements, also if they like tea/coffee brought in the morning or to make the drink in their own room or show them where to find the necessaries downstairs. If a proposal is made for anything good or necessary, make a note and follow it up.

How to cope with very pleasant guest wished on you by a friend because he had a business appointment in the area, but forgets to write a thank you letter. After about a week to 10 days, write asking if they left behind a pair of size 8 shoes for a large man or size 14 ones for a small man. This will elicit a thank you without causing offence. You can also start the letter by asking if they got home safely.

My grandfather, who was extremely forgetful and rather deaf failed to hear the door being answered by a maid. She had gone upstairs to find my grandmother, who was out. My grandmother had in fact told my grandfather that guests were expected. He heard voices in the hall, went out, saw the suitcases and said "Oh dear, I'm sorry you have to leave so soon. I will call a cab." This he did. The cab arrived swiftly and bore them away without demur.

How to look after a Paying Guest

Be sure to have their correct names to hand to save embarrassment. Check that guest room has a bedside light that works; fresh bed linen and towels and is warm and aired. Tell your guest how to find the bathroom. Ideally they should have their own. It is welcoming to have a "hospitality tray" in the guest room with a kettle, etc. Sometimes guests appreciate some privacy – others like to be "part of the family". Tell them that they are welcome at family breakfast time.

HOUSEHOLD

If you have a routine, rather boring task put a photo of a friend or family near where you are for that task. If you have an often used one which takes too long because something needs mending, altering or moving, make the change as soon as possible and you will be grateful every day.
Preventing build-up of lime with white wine vinegar: White vinegar is acidic and mildly disinfectant. It can be used to clean sinks, windows and any surface. It is good for de-scaling kettles and irons and for getting the lime scale off the ends of taps where it can be brushed on briskly with a stiff toothbrush, also for scrubbing the lime scale off the back of the loo pan where hard water has dripped on. It can be used to clean upholstery when diluted 50:50 with water. If used to clean fabric, always apply to the back of the fabric. It is very good for cleaning off cat pee from upholstery, carpets and clothing.
Kettles can also be de-scaled with a metal descaler. It is a small metal coil which attracts lime to itself thus sparing the element.
To glue different surfaces together use Liquid Glue gun available at Wicks in Yeovil or Bridgewater.
Play music while you work. Tie a sprig of rosemary up with string and hang over hot bath tap. It gives a lovely scent and saves money on bubble bath, etc.
Keep a small sewing box with essentials in the kitchen.
If you cannot remember that to close a tap or lid you twist it clockwise and vice versa, use the adage "Righty tighty, lefty loosey".
Brooms: storing head up prevents damage to bristles.
Extra large table napkins (50cm x 50cm): These are hard to source but can be made from checked linen tea towels cut into squares.
To remove objects from difficult narrow space, get a pair of long (12") forceps available from Taunton Anglers. Hang them in the kitchen. They have dozens of uses – removing things from behind radiators and furniture, objects out of boiling water or clamping things together, etc.
Use nail varnish to distinguish similar containers or to mark an opening point on bottles, pots, boxes etc.
To get a glass stopper out of a glass jar or bottle, immerse in warm water then ease it out.

Appliances To keep oven clean, smother sides with paste of bicarbonate of soda.

To defrost freezer, put oblong bowl of hot water in bottom of freezer. For manual defrosting use a scraper from a car accessories shop. They are cheaper than the ones from household suppliers and can fit between the bars under freezer drawers.

To keep washing machine smelling fresh rub the sides with ½ lemon and put on final rinse programme.

Cutlery, crockery and utensils To remove tea stains from cups and mugs, use a Magic Eraser Block obtainable from Lakeland.

Chipped heavy cut glass: File down with fine round file till chip is smooth. For final smoothness wrap emery paper around the file and continue. To tell if a glass is safe in the dishwasher feel over the rim and if there is a definite ridge it is 99% safe in the dishwasher.

For safety, put corks on ends of sharp scissors.

Mending china: Hold the article together with sellotape while glue sets or prop it up in a drawer or stand in dry sand or a mixture of the first two methods.

Use Milliput to fill gaps and when dry cover with car enamel or a mixture of car enamel and a good coloured bike enamel. White car enamel can be obtained at a garage with a car body shop. (Take your own small paint tin for paint to be decanted into.)

More professional menders - make sure to use a slow acting epoxy glue. This gives more time for fine adjustment. To make sure that cracks are properly aligned run the top of a pencil across the crack. If there is a slight click the edges are not properly aligned. If several pieces of a plate are involved this may take some time as each readjustment throws another piece out. Use woven fabric tape, as used for carpets, instead of Sellotape. Unlike Sellotape it does not stretch.

Freezer Small plastic bottles may be obtained from Ikea or large Tesco. Even smaller ones may be purchased from takeaway restaurants (often used by Chinese or Thai restaurants). Save the ones used by you (should be sterilised.) Label everything well and keep list on side of the freezer fixed with travel magnet. Score off as used.

Jewellery How to look after pearls: Wearing pearls gives them natural moisture but wipe them gently occasionally with a damp cloth too. Don't spray perfume or hairspray near pearls - the alcohol base damages them.

Don't wear them in the bath, which rots the string, or when asleep, which damages it. Store in a silk pouch and restring every few years.

Oven gloves Get a strong magnet and secure to oven gloves by covering with a patch of strong material. Hang on side of oven or freezer. Available from Hawkins Bazaar or similar company.

Pest prevention Cover fruit with a fly net. Use old fashioned fly swat and fly papers or a UV fly zapper switched on at night. Chemical fly killers may be dangerous. For spiders and other creepy crawlies, scatter fresh conkers on the floors of each room affected.

Silver cleaning: Use a Goddard's long term silver cleaning cloth to give cutlery a quick rub as you put it away. Then use foam cleaner occasionally. Be careful not to throw away the plastic disc provided in the pot. A standard silver cleaner such as Silvo, brushed on with an old toothbrush, is best for ornate silver. Silver photo frames: either remove glass and photo and protect velvet backing with a piece of paper or slip a piece of glossy magazine paper between the frame and the glass. Silver dip can remove some of the silver so beware with silver plate. With antique silver take care not to rub too hard on the hallmark. Wear gloves or clean hands afterwards with a Lady Jane fine cleaning pad. Store silver mugs in paper bag covered by plastic bag (stops light and air)

Washing up

Draining plates after washing: Put on far end of drainer. This saves lifting later ones over them.

Removing stains from decanters: put in a good tablespoon of sand and a little water and shake vigorously alternatively, use a Milton sterilising tablet (used for babies' bottles).

To keep a thermos flask clean: Fill with cold water immediately after use and keep it for a few hours. If much stain is found after this, add a little sodium bicarbonate or ½ tablet of Steradent (used to sterilise false teeth) to the water and leave overnight. (*False teeth can be an embarrassment. A guest at a royal garden party was once looking at the apple trees and found a pair of false teeth deeply embedded in a meringue lodged in the cleft of a low branch.*)

Dirty saucepan: Steep it in bio detergent overnight; cover with salt overnight; put sodium bicarbonate and water in the pan and boil; or put dead deciduous leaves and water in the pan and boil.

Frying pan: As above or leave in the garden and the slugs will clean it.
Cleaning non-stick pans: Use a Lady Jane pad.
Roasting pan. After gravy has been made in a pan, put some water and detergent in the pan and boil it gently on the hob to disperse residue.
To get vegetable remnants out of saucepan before they stick use a soft, clean washing up brush.

Bathrooms and loos
To stop noxious smells, pull the chain before standing up. Occasional examination of stool is wise. Any persistent blood, black or very pale bulky stool should be reported to your Doctor.
Encourage children to dry their feet before stepping onto the bathmat. Store soap in a good ridged soap dish.
To get rid of hairs down a plughole: Fill it with bio washing powder.
Energy and water saving: Emptying the loo cistern takes a huge amount of water. For an old cistern insert a hippo bag which displaces water thus reducing the volume each time. If buying a new cistern get a dual flow one.

Books
To distinguish dark books, such as diaries, put strips of bright insulating tape on the spine in different colours.
When lending books, place a card saying to whom they have been lent and the date in the gap the book leaves on the shelf. Put a reminder note in your diary, one month ahead, and keep a list at the back. It is the ones who say they never forget who generally do.

Carpets
To clean: Use hot water and lots of detergent. Froth it and throw the foam all over the carpet. Leave overnight until dry then vacuum.
To remove stain made by a dog's puddle, soak it up with newspaper, as much as possible, as soon as possible, then cover patch with sparkling water, fizzy lemonade, or soda water, then leave to dry naturally. Red wine spilt on carpets: pour white wine on it at once or thick salt.
For dimples in carpet left by heavy furniture legs : Put ice cubes in them.
To prevent wet paws or shoes from making the floor wet and muddy use Turtle mats, they really work. Find them at turtlemat.co.uk

Clothes
Taking fluff off clothes: Use Sellotape wound round your hand.
If a pair of shoes is too tight fill a plastic bag with water leaving a little air in it. Seal well and leave for about 24 hours in the freezer. Do not overfill the bag.
If clothes are not used for 2 years give them away or, if they are haute couture or best quality and you have enough room, keep them until your child or grandchild would like them.
Moth prevention: Use a lavender bag or a well cleaned shoe polish tin with holes punched in its lid containing smashed up moth balls or rings. Hang a pheromone device such as Zero moth treatment obtainable from John Lewis inside and outside a wardrobe.
Tying shoe laces: Wind lace round then again (double overhand). Make a loose bow but put the loop through a second time, then tighten (see illustration). It will not come undone.

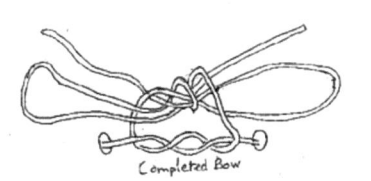

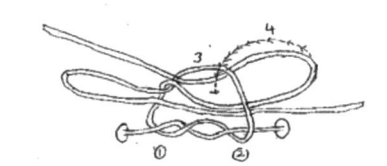

Lining drawers
Keep a lavender bag in a drawer for scent and to deter moths.
Line drawers with folded newspaper 2 sheets thick. Put the paper in the drawer, turn up the excess paper and press the fold down then turn the whole paper over. For bow-fronted drawers the fold must be well marked with a pen, then turn the paper over and press the fold down. This saves money as well as providing interesting reading in the future but beware:
A precocious 4 year old boy known to the editor emerged from the airing cupboard one day asking, "Mum, what's incest?"
Washing clothes:
Do up a duvet before washing. This stops small items getting inside.
After washing washable loose covers, replace while still slightly damp – they are easier to fit.

When hanging clothes on the line: Peg a shirt up by the bottom with the open front facing the wind which then billows the sleeves out. Turn trouser pockets inside out.

Washing woollens:
See also washing wool under stains
Wash in lukewarm water and keep wet for a minimum time. Put a few drops of Eucalyptus oil in the rinsing water. This replaces the natural lanolin. Spin in a free standing spinner. These spin much faster than the spin in a large machine ie 2,800 revs per minute compared to 1,600 revs per minute. *Two varieties are available at Sparkworld in Martock: a pump spin dryer which pumps via a tube into the sink or a drain spin dryer which requires a bucket or basin under the drainer.* Pull gently into shape and dry on a flat towel. Never use bio powder to remove stains in wool. It eats the wool. For a cashmere woollen item that has shrunk in the wash, treat immediately by rinsing in hair shampoo then follow by washing in lukewarm water and putting a few drops of Eucalyptus oil *(Tip given but not absolutely proven.)*
To make angora (or any similar fabric) fluffy again: Place in fridge for about 30 minutes.
For easy ironing, put the washing machine on a short spin.

Ironing.
Use a good iron and board. Always test heat before starting. Test iron on a corner of the fabric in an area usually not visible. Beware that silk can float up to a hot iron. If called to the door or telephone switch the iron off. If the flex becomes frayed cover it with insulating tape. Never steam iron a woollen garment. **To iron a shirt**: G*iven by a housekeeper at the London Hilton* spread the whole yolk out flat and iron it. Next, do the whole of the back then the sleeves, then the sides and last the collar. This prevents creases on the top of the yolk and on the front and collar as you move the garment around.
If left-handed get a cordless iron and descale it from time to time if necessary.
For easy ironing – put the washing machine on a short spin especially after washing woollens.

Emergencies

Fire: Make sure you know how to open all locked windows especially upstairs. Have fire blankets and fire extinguishers at strategic places and make sure that the extinguishers are replaced when out of date. Check fire and smoke alarms regularly.

Leave all doors closed when you leave the house empty. In case of fire, close all doors. Cover your face with a towel and keep head low as you exit. An emergency rope can be made by tying sheets together.

Away from home: Carry your mobile phone with you at all times. (The editor was once locked in a hotel loo and had to phone a friend to alert the hotel.)

If trapped in a room because the door handle has fallen off taking the spindle with it on the other side, jam a pencil, biro or sliver of wood into the hole (pad out with a tissue if necessary) and wind a length of material such as a scarf round the new spindle clockwise leaving a long enough length to pull down and rotate spindle. (You may have to sacrifice your bra, knicker elastic or pants.) The editor discovered this method when trapped by a door leading to the roof of an isolated house. Fortunately there were splinters of wood in the attic and some pipes were lagged with rags. Some door handles have locking knobs which can be accidentally pressed or a button which needs twisting.

Furniture

White water marks on wood furniture: Rub with methylated spirit or with the flat side of a walnut kernel. A paste of wood ash and water, rubbed in gently, also works but it is mildly abrasive. For biro marks on furniture rub in a little milk.

Scratches in furniture: Rub with walnut if it is a similar colour or a brazil nut kernal, or rub in matching brown shoe polish. For deep scratches use scratch cover or, for deeper scratches, scratch filler available at Whites in Wells or other hardware shops.

For any wood furniture (not French polished) that needs refurbishing or removal of blackness accrued with age use the following mixtures: equal parts boiled linseed oil, white spirit and meths. Rub the surface with fine wire wool working in line with the wood grain.

Furniture Repairs: These are best done by an expert or take classes.

Chair Maintenance: Always lift chairs by the seat - never by the back which loosens the joint. Take the joint or break apart. Clean the exposed surfaces then repair, apply wood glue and clamp. Tools needed: a sharp chisel, mallet, adjustable clamps, wood glue and binding material.
Woodworm: Paint with Rentokil and allowed to sink in. Repeat if necessary.

Office/Study

Computer care given by two computer gurus
When getting rid of a computer make sure everything is destroyed including the waste bin. Completely destroy the hard drive. This can be done with a very strong magnet, but better still, get a knowledgeable expert to do it for you. A clean hard drive can be installed by an expert. This should help to prevent your identity being stolen.
ALWAYS back up and, if you don't know how to, find out. To protect computer from damage by electricity supply surge, plug into surge protection extension lead. This is supposed to give some protection against lightning strike but unplug if there is lightning. A surge protector is as much use as a chocolate teapot. When cleaning a laptop screen turn off the computer. It can damage the screen and don't press hard on the screen which can fracture. Use spray on window cleaner but spray it onto a soft cloth not the screen. The fluid can dribble down and wreck the electronics or clean with the cloth used for specs or binoculars. Liquids can permanently damage the C drive. Use flat bottomed mugs or glasses – avoid wine glasses.
To prevent theft of money through statements, receipts and letters disposed of in the wheelie bin: Shred the documents or cut or tear the corner or strip with sensitive information and add to the compost.
To prevent phone scam, never give your details to someone purporting to be from your bank. Put phone down and ring your bank after 10 minutes to verify. If you phone immediately they may just have left their phone off the hook and you are still connected to them. You may hear a medley of other authentic sounds in the background but you are not through to your bank. If someone charming phones you, saying that you have won or inherited a large sum of money and asks for your bank details so that it can be paid in, don't give it. It's a scam.

The same applies if a hospital sends a letter purporting to be from a student needing money to complete their course. Phoning the hospital will reveal that no such student exists.
Leaving a message on an answer phone Make the message as short as possible and say your number slowly and/ or repeat it.
Requesting a reference When asking for a reference from someone who is not a personal friend enclose an S A E. Teachers in schools and colleges and university lecturers get inundated with such requests.
Mobile phone charger : If the charger cable will not stay in the phone because the end of the cable near to the phone is weak, strengthen with the wire coil removed from an old biro.

Wire from biro used to hold parts of mobile phone charger's wire from finally falling apart.

Unruly Sellotape: keep the end of the sellotape just to one side of roll or cut a 4mm wide strip from credit card and put across its end leaving a 4mm overlap to secure the end. To find the end of tape that has stuck, run your tongue around the roll – it is more sensitive than fingers and will detect a ridge.
If something is too good to be true, it is too good to be true. There is no such thing as a free lunch.
Rubber that has stopped working: Rub hard on a rough stone wall.
Automatic pencils some have rubbers that hardly work. Make a note of the ones that do, e.g. Cobra and Zebra and stick to them.
To keep clean a photocopier plate: Use a little meths on a clean rag.
Keyring: Include a small torch and a Sentinel tag (if you subscribe to Sentinel then anyone finding your keys only has to drop them into any post box and they will be returned to you. Sentinel will also alert your bank if any of your credit cards are stolen or help to return lost luggage.
Telephone calls: To stop nuisance calls politely try "I'm sorry I'm not allowed to answer calls like this" or "Parlez-vous français?". Chinese or Russian may be better. Some people, perhaps rather unkindly, leave the telephone off the hook so that the caller cannot use the line.
If calls are an extreme nuisance play along with it, get all the contact details of the firm and then send solicitor's letter.

Junk mail: You may be tempted to stop all junk mail but remember that it forms a large part of Royal Mail's income so you might think again if you want to keep the service going.

Organising a new kitchen.
Think of the way you move around the kitchen as you work (the ergonomics). Have everything to hand for each task e.g., dirty dishes on one side of the sink above the dishwasher and clean things on the other. Put plates on the drainer filling the far side first.
Hang up as many implements as possible. Cull redundant instruments regularly.
When ordering a new kitchen double check that the colour of worktops in the image sent by the firm is what you ordered.

Plumbing
Turn off the water if going on holiday. (*The previous owners of a house failed to turn it off before leaving. On arrival, the new owners found a study door would not open because of a solid sheet of ice. The house was not insured.*)
If a radiator goes cold or cold only at the top open the valve at the top with a radiator key and hold an old rag under the valve in case it spurts out water as it fills. This is known as "bleeding" the radiator. When turning off a radiator turn it back ½ a turn. This prevents the tap from jamming.
In summer turn the heating on from time to time to prevent air locks and (if gas) to make sure there are no leaks.
Hang a radiator key by a piece of string on any radiator that tends to trap air.
If a radiator a long way from the boiler tends to stay cold despite bleeding, turn off the boiler and all the other radiators. Restart the boiler and the air is driven out of the rogue radiator. You can then turn on all the other radiators.
Loo cistern: If you need to flush the loo urgently e.g. there is a queue outside and the cistern is slow to complete filling, lift the lid off the cistern and press the ball valve down to increase water flow until the valve closes easily.

Saving energy
Installing solar or photovoltaic panels makes sense especially if likely to live in the house for several years. Find a good local supplier. Ask other people in area who installed their system. Be aware that any shade from nearby trees

will diminish their efficiency. Take installers instructions on use and safety carefully. For photovoltaic panels, find out how to disarm the system in case of fire. (There should be a red button to push.) Inform your Electricity Company promptly when the system is installed.   Use washing and dishwashing machines during sunlight hours. In winter, if hot water is only available in day, save some in a thermos flask for washing up after dusk.

Saving the planet
To save money and the planet, keep the plastic bags from junk and other mail and use for your own mail or for saving non-meat items in the fridge.

Saving water
When washing hands it is more economical to put water into the basin than to wash under a running tap. A bath may be more economical with water if shared by family members than two or three showers. A power shower may use as much water as a small bath if it is kept running for a long time. If too much water is used in a kettle, save it in a vacuum flask.
Car washing: Washing a car at a garage saves water as it is all recycled. If washing at home two buckets, one soapy the other clean, may be enough. Work from the top down. Keep lights clean and have car cleaned underneath in spring to remove corroding salt.

Shopping
Ask the till attendant to use only one knot to close plastic bags. Double knots hinder re-use.
If visiting a friend after shopping place any frozen or chilled food in their fridge or freezer but leave car keys on top of them (ditto if not in fridge). When leaving the house recite: Wally, ticky money, keys, testicles, spectacles, anything esticles (e.g. mobile phone).
Use bulk buys on special deals. Watch for offers in daily papers. Smile whenever possible – it makes a huge difference to staff. Don't try to shop if you are running for a bus. Decide which you want to do and do it. Take everything with you.
A young lady was lucky enough to be asked to a royal function which required the wearing of a tiara. She borrowed her mother's which was kept

in the bank, went shopping and kept it with her safely in a plastic bag. In her haste she left it at the till. On getting home she realised her mistake, rang the store and said, "Did you find something strange at the till an hour ago?" The reply was "Oh, are you the lady that left the toy tiara behind? Yes, we have it."

Judging value: Beware, sometimes small packets are cheaper than one large one.

Loo rolls

This is complicated. At the time of enquiry it was:

Andrex Quilted 9 pack	£4.99	150 sheets per roll = 3p per sheet	110mm x 125mm
Andrex Classic 9 pack	£4.50	221 sheets per roll = 2p per sheet	110mm x 124mm
Tesco Quilted 9 pack	£4.00	176 sheets per roll = 2p per sheet	124mm x 105mm
Tesco Luxury 9 pack	£3.55	220 sheets per roll = 2p per sheet	124mm x 105mm
Tesco Value 6 pack	£1.00	200 sheets per roll = ½ p per sheet	115mm x 96mm

But cheaper rolls are much thinner and you may need 2 sheets where 1 of the more expensive type will do.

During WW2 loo paper, which was not soft had printed messages on the sheets such as 'Now wash your hands'. One naval ship trying to economise had the useful suggestion 'Use both sides'.

Are they environment friendly? The cores of all loo rolls are recycled. When asked about the use of bleach, both firms stated that the paper was made from FSC approved sources. Andrex refused to give any info re. bleach. Tesco said that they had a legal responsibility to do so. *(FSC seems to indicate substances used per weight of paper)*

Stains.

Biro. Put a cloth behind it. Spray it with hair spray and leave it for a short while. The stain spreads – don't panic, rinse and it goes. Fatty spots. Wash with soap or baby shampoo. Tar: soften with butter then wash.

Tea stains: fresh stains – soak in a warm solution of biological detergent; old dry stains – soak in washing soda dissolved in boiling water (1oz soda per pint water) for several hours then rinse out. When dry try using meths (not tried by donor). For remaining stain soak in strong bleach (50:50 in water). Test small area of fabric for colour fastness first.

Oil: Use petrol. Paint: Treat immediately with turpentine then wash.

Red wine: Dry off with a cloth then use Vanish (test first) or cover in salt or apply white wine.

Grease on clothes: Put brown paper or several layers of paper towel on both sides and iron the grease away.

To remove lily pollen stain from clothes. Put lots of talcum powder on it then blow it off again or wind sellotape round your hand, sticky side out, and gently dab it off then lift it off with small hand held vacuum cleaner.

A husband when ironing his wife's borrowed white stole for a wedding managed to get it stained with lily pollen. He panicked but the bride who was there said **not to touch it or rub it in**. She got some talcum powder and dusted the stain with it. After 10 minutes she shook it out and the stain disappeared as if by magic. His wife was completely unaware of the drama.

Remove Tipp-ex with Meths. Rub grease off wallpaper with dry bread.

To remove wax from the floor, carpet or garment cover it with absorbent paper and iron.

To remove chewing gum from the floor put an ice cube on it and remove when it has hardened. For a garment, place it in the fridge until the gum has hardened.

To kill moth or louse or flea infestations on a garment place it in the freezer for ½ an hour.

To get rid of any stain on fabric or a hard surface: Put washing up liquid on the surface, rub in and leave for a long time then wash in cold or tepid water.

HOW TO . . .

How to help a refugee.
Refer him/her to the local refugee centre. Introduce them to a suitable church or mosque.
Introduce them to a local market where they may get familiar food and to cheap English food such as carrots. If they are lucky enough to have a food allowance it is barely sufficient for basic needs and food tokens don't help them to buy market food.
If torture is suspected the refugee centre may help or better, refer to the Medical Foundation for the Treatment of Torture or one of its branches. Children may be given a book to read in English.
Be aware that they may suffer from Post Traumatic Stress disorder with nightmares; panic attacks (a racing heart or fainting); fear of police in uniform; irrational anger with violence and a tendency to alcoholism or drug abuse to alleviate their terrors.
For military persons suffering from stress, refer to "Combat Stress." Long walks are often helpful for stress. Beware of the suicide risk.

How to make a difference
If joining a political activist group check your facts first. Use social media such as "Hello my name is" started by Kate Grainger which has had huge success.
Start a charity in aid of someone who has died and use it to make life better for others or contribute to an existing charity.
When shopping, if no local food is available such as apples, complain to a manager.
Support your local theatre and library, village shop and post office or any other amenity threatened with closure.

How to be a feminist
Be welcoming to all women from all walks of life, creeds, races and sexualities. Be willing to talk about your own experiences. Have a safe place for others to talk about their situation.

How to help farmers
Close gates. Do not enter a field if the bull is with the cows. Keep to the paths and keep dogs on leads. (This is especially important when there is hay or grass for silage lying on the ground. Dog poo can leave parasites and bacteria on the fodder. The dog is effectively pooing on the cattle's dinner

plate.) Lobby politicians about the low price of milk in the supermarkets. In the last year dairy farmers have lost 25% of their income but the cost of fuel, insurance, sterilizing agents for the milking parlour etc. have soared.

How to help your plumber in case of flood
Know where the water stop valve is and turn it off. Know where the electricity and gas meters are and switch off electricity and turn off gas.
If the flood is near any appliance make sure that the manuals of any appliances are available. Make sure that you have good access especially in the airing cupboard.
Leave the plumber to put his own carpet protector down on the stairs and other carpets – they stick to the carpet but yours could slip.
Give him a cup of tea.

How to speak to Taxi drivers.
Know your destination. Be polite and friendly - they usually are. Take everything with you when you get out. *(One elderly clergyman left his favourite Bible in a London cab. The cabby came to his door and returned the Bible the same night.)*

How to help your Postman.
Ensure that you have the correct address and postcode; have a letterbox large enough for A4 envelopes at a reasonable height. Keep biting dogs indoors. Postmen are not allowed to carry titbits any more.

How to speak to Tradesmen.
Be polite and friendly to tradesmen. They often know a lot more than you do.

How to care for Old and Long Case Clocks: Given by a master clock repairer
Service regularly – yearly for long case clocks and keep wound up. (If a clock is left unwound the oil will gradually harden leaving it difficult to clean.)
Insure well and don't put them in direct sunlight which causes intermittent expansion of the metal parts. It is also bad for wooden cases. Use beeswax for wooden cases, NEVER aerosols.

How to run a good Lawn Hunt Meet: (Absolutely not run on a lawn) *from the horse's mouth*
Find out the likely number of riders from the hunt secretary and have plenty of small unbreakable glasses ready. Put glasses and drink on a table and protect food from vacuuming hounds. Lay on lots of drink – port (the cheapest possible), soft drinks, and, for brownie points, whisky and may be in milk for the Master huntsman and whippers-in but hide the bottle from

others. Don't hand out any food or drink until hounds arrive. Serve the Master and hunt staff first and then other riders. Food - ginger biscuits, fruitcake in small pieces, small sausage rolls plus small sausages and chips for children – all manageable with one hand. Beware of free loaders taking excess drink. Recruit lots of volunteer waiters.

How to fly your own plane.
Safer than riding a horse and you don't have to clear up after it.

How to open your house to the public: *Given by the owners of an 18th century Dorset house and a county Fermanagh house and an Edwardian house owner*
Join the Historic Houses Association. Visit other house owners and share ideas. To fund the enterprise be entrepreneurial. As well as weddings, have events to suit your interests and the locality, concerts, festivals, talks and themed weekends. Make contact with the local orchestra and university; also, NACF and NADFAS. Develop outhouses to let, facilities for outdoor sports and games, e.g. fishing or have a butterfly house etc. Learn from your guests.

Arriving in a new job.
Get to know the names of pupils, colleagues, employees, parishioners, etc. as soon as possible and in as friendly a way as possible.

How to start your own company. *Given by a green tourism company owner*
Be ready to work hard. It is 99% hard work 1% luck and like having a baby, exhausting at first but see the results later. Write a business plan, including your likely clients, partners, competitors, suppliers, employees, etc. Hope for the best but be ready for the worst. Find a mentor and meet regularly for a disinterested opinion.

HOW TO BE A GOOD ...

How to be a good Architect *given by an award winning architect*
Be a visionary and be able to inspire potential clients with your vision. Be good at maths and dimensions also at drawing, despite the use of computer generated images.   This Architect went to give a bid for a potential contract, the computer failed but he won the contract partly because he had excellent, hand-drawn plans.

How to be a good Automobile Rescue Patrol Man
Keep calm. Always listen to advice from others.

How to be a good Baker.
Do not hurry.

How to be a good Banker g*iven by the former chairman of a leading English bank.*
Never forget that you are handling other people's money. You should first safeguard depositors then promote growth by constructive lending. When in doubt between these two err on the side of caution. When things go wrong always explain and always apologise. Never be arrogant as however big your bank you rank behind firstly primary producers then manufacturing and services. Never get too close to government. Choosing a worthwhile application for a loan needs experience and gut feeling. One in three applications for a loan is successful and it takes 5 years for a business to be successful.

How to be a good independent Bookshop Owner:
Giving good customer service is paramount. Offer a wide range of books and a quick ordering service. Stay in touch with your customers. Encourage reading clubs and offer them a discount.
Be intuitive – a customer may not know the title or author and maybe only some part of the story.

How to be a good Bookshop Customer:
Know the title and author of the book (or at least the title.). When asking for a children's book the reading age is more important e.g. what other books are they enjoying? For teenagers there are "crossover books" which are intended for adults but enjoyed by teenagers too e.g. "Game of Thrones" by George Martin.

How to be a good Bus Conductor
Enjoy people and your job. Know the route and in a city other routes.
How to be a good Car Mechanic: *Given by a Car Mechanic in Somerton*
Take a course at a college or university. Have the knack: without this the knowledge is virtually useless. Have common sense e.g. for lifting heavy loads which can be extremely dangerous. If you don't know how it works don't try to fix it.
How to be a good Cinema Usherette
Be polite even when someone is rude to you. It is usually about the price of ice creams (£3.50 per pot) or about the seats.
How to run a Charity
Never give up. Play to people's strengths. You gain much more than you give.
How to be a good Clock Repairer *given by a master clock repairer*
A good clock repairer needs experience and training (best done through apprenticeship), enthusiasm and the ability to do fine engineering. The skills are often handed from father to son. The craft seems to go with good humour.

Agriculture
How to be a good Farmer *given by an organic farmer who also has an excellent farm shop in the village of Pitney between Langport and Somerton*
Treat the soil like your wife, with care and respect. You are in a long term relationship. Always carry baler twine and a pocket knife. It is amazing the problems you can solve with these things. Never attempt a risky job on your own. Too many lives have been lost because there has been no-one present to help or raise the alarm. If deciding when it's warm enough to plant spring crops take your trousers off and sit on the ground and put yourself in the soil's place. Respect the Mother-Offspring bond. Do everything you can to aid it at birth and don't come between them later on.
Don't bottle up your worries. Talk to someone who can help. The Farming Network Community (0845 3679990) are very good listeners.
How to be a good Farmer's Wife
This depends on the size and type of farm e.g. for a **Large contract farm:** you may need to do a lot of office work, answering the telephone etc. One farmer's wife was warned before she got married "Don't volunteer to learn to drive a tractor or milk a cow or one day you may become a necessity".

Gone are the days of large numbers of workers needing lunch but for some farms there will be a few men to be fed or, if running a shoot, several.

On a small dairy farm Be a good intermediary; talk to Defra when necessary; fill in complicated protocol forms; be present when there are veterinary inspections; fill in forms giving exact details; do tagging; make sure that phone is manned at all times.

On a small arable farm be flexible. Have a go at anything. Work with the weather. Where necessary do tractor work.

How to be a good Forester *Given by a former chairman of the Forestry and Timber Association*

Work from nature using natural processes. Adopt a low cost, low intervention approach. Remember that the wood that pays is the wood that stays. Do not remove more volume than the incremental growth since the previous intervention. Leave the best quality trees to provide seed for future generations. Britain could have lost WWI through a lack of timber needed for pit props in coal mines more than bullets (no munitions without the energy from coal). Clear filling was then introduced. Woods provide timber, habitats for flora and fauna, health and recreational benefits, plus enhanced landscapes and reduced flooding risks. Good foresters no longer clear fell. But take out the largest trees intermittently – leaving holes in the canopy and allowing natural regeneration of the trees and flora.

Armed Forces

How to be a good Naval Officer *given by a retired Submarine Captain RN*
As with both other services you need intelligence, initiative, integrity and common sense. He told of advice given to him by his commanding officer, another Captain RN: "Behave like a gentleman, fear God and honour the Queen." He mentioned an incident in 1971 when there was a dangerous explosion in a submarine's battery. An immediate inquiry showed that a vital valve had not opened. A petty officer instantly and with great moral courage owned up to it being his fault. This saved all other 20-25 submarines in the fleet being recalled for inspection.

Tips added by another retired captain for a novice sailor
Learn the difference between a ship and a boat. On joining a new ship explore every corner. If asked a question to which you do not know the answer say "I don't know but I will try to find out" not just "I don't know."

Care for your brothers in arms and study the Navy's glorious history. Aim for the highest possible standards. When in foreign ports make friends – you can represent your country's good qualities.

A visiting Admiral asked a sailor standing by a lifebelt "What are your duties?" He replied "If a sailor goes overboard I raise the alarm and throw him the belt." "And if an officer falls overboard?" "Which h'orficer Sir?" *(Told to the editor by a retired 1st Sea Lord)*

How to be a good Wren Officer

Do what you are told. Never talk about politics or religion and <u>never</u> volunteer – you may fall for the trap "Who plays the piano?" "I do." "OK, you'll clean the latrines."

How to be a good Army Officer

You need intelligence, initiative, integrity, self-confidence and common sense. Soldiers expect you to be honest, wise, fair, a good example, firm fit and professional. A young TA officer who served in Afghanistan said that you would need to have integrity, compassion and bravery and that he would follow anyone of whatever rank who had these qualities. You also need the ability to inspire and boost morale e.g. Col Tim Collins' eve of battle speech to his battalion in Iraq in 2003. Besides intuition, loyalty to your comrades, enthusiasm, a sense of humour and determination there is also the need to have courage to change or cancel a plan when other factors materialise e.g. Napoleon's disastrous retreat from Moscow in 1814 and the decision to carry on with the Arnhem operation after the 255 Panzer divisions had come into the area.

How to be a good RAF Officer *given by a retired RAF Officer*

You need integrity, wisdom and leadership qualities. To have all 3 qualities is unusual and to act with humility and fairness as well is truly exceptional. These parameters would apply to any of the services but as the late Archbishop Robert Runcie once said to the editor "No one who lacks a sense of humour should be put in charge of anything". Robert Runcie had all these qualities and was the first to admit if he was in the wrong. The editor had once to apologise to him for a grave mistake and he said "That's nothing. Last week I failed to notice a typing error in a letter which I had signed. It was about a worthy charity and ended 'You must by no means support this excellent charity.' I had assumed it said 'All' and not 'No' and we had to write over a hundred letters of apology"

Church

How to be a good Bishop *from a retired Bishop*
A Bishop's wife, words and actions should be a credible witness to the Gospel of Jesus Christ. He/she must care for his/her clergy but the people must always come first. Nobody who needs or longs to be a Bishop needs to be one.

How to be a Bishop's wife *Account and tip given by a retired bishop's wife*
You need a strong back as you will spend a lot of time moving house. Develop the art of changing clothes quickly (it is princes to dustmen). Bishops are given a health check before taking up their appointment. Their wives are not – curious! When going to a function e.g. confirmation, no one will know who you are so say "I am the Bishop's wife. Would you like me to sit in a special place?"

How to be a good Minister
Love God – He is the whole point of your work. Play to your strengths and focus on what you do well and what you are passionate about. Love people – your congregation may sometimes seem difficult but they are only human and if they know that you care they will forgive you for much. Love yourself – you are only human. Take time off and have a life beyond the parish. It is better for everyone.

How to be a good Clergy Wife
This is no longer a common role. Many clergy wives have another occupation. Clergy and their wives are often abused both physically and mentally by the general public and sadly by their own parishioners. If you are abused seek help from a diocesan adviser on pastoral care. Know yourself. Expect as much of your own energy and talent as any other lay person.

How to be a good Congregation
Share the load and enjoy church. Smile, welcome strangers, laugh at the bad jokes and don't take offence when things go wrong. Care for your ministers – they are human too and have feelings, make mistakes and have bad days like everyone. Never say, "I know it's your day off but I thought I'd call you before you go off." "We love children in church but can we stop them being noisy?" "You can't move Mrs Jones's pew." "We tried that once and it didn't work."

How to be a good Town Chaplain
Listen and pray. Don't try to fix what can't be fixed, such as marriage breakdown.

How to be a good Church Warden
Be on good terms with your church architect, your archdeacon, your incumbent and PCC and be tolerant and kind. As always rely on God. At a WI fete the ladies were surprised when a man won the 'squeeze a lemon' competition. He remarked, "But I am a church treasurer and I'm used to getting money out of stones".

Education

How to be a good Teacher
Get to know your children, their names and interests. Always remember that there are children in front of you who are more intelligent than you. Always admit you are wrong if you make a mistake. Use the eyes in the back of your head. Develop a teacher's stare! Don't get really cross but simulate being so and "forget" it the next day. Help them to reach their potential according to their ability. Have fun.

How to be a good Chairman of School Governors *given by a former chairman and present governor*
Remember that your head teacher has one of the most demanding and lonely jobs possible and be supportive even when you disagree. Remember and remind your board colleagues that a school is not a business and that, while it must try to stay in the black, its primary purpose is the good education of its pupils. Remember that knowledge of the history of the school is invaluable in giving a wide perspective to its future direction.

How to be a good Boarding School Teacher *given by a retired head teacher.*
As with any school, boarding should be a happy time when life long friends are made. Do a bit of mothering for younger children; though there are other pastoral staff who do most of this. Gently remind them about changing clothes, personal hygiene and being appropriately dressed for lessons, hair tied back, etc. Make sure prep is done on time – at school there is no "dog" to eat it. Watch out for those who cannot get to sleep in dormitories and get too tired to work well. Be alert to those who arrive at class upset; incidents however trivial need care and compassion. Good or bad news received during daytime impacts more as it comes by email or a phone call rather than

face to face. It can prey on a child's mind. (*Head teachers often know a good two years in advance if a divorce is looming.*) Allow good fun and play time. School is their home.
(*When the Navy was stationed at Roedean Girls School during the war they liked the notice in the dormitories which stated, "If a mistress is required during the night, ring the bell."*)
The classes in a **remand home** are always small (10-12 max). Think of what is in it for them. Reward good behaviour and attention e.g. they are promised a 10 minute football break or time on a computer. One remand home headmaster invented this game: At the start of the class say, "I am going to show you some money in my hand and at the end of class anyone who has behaved well may join in. Whoever knows the exact amount will be given the money." Then show them an assortment of coins for 3 seconds.

Entertainment
How to be an Aspiring Actor *given by a veteran amateur actor and producer*
Learn your lines. Turn up on time for rehearsals and don't fall for the gag when another actor hands you an unwanted egg or answers a phone call vital to the plot and hands it to you saying, 'It's for you dear'.
How to be a good Film Director *given by one such*
Find a work placement from an independent company. Start as a researcher and hope for a break. You must be a good writer. To write a proposal: The first line must arouse interest and must be brief and contain things that can be visualised. Choose the correct target e.g. Channel 5 for a generally popular theme and Channel 1 on ITV for sitcom and 5 for the intelligentsia and submit it to a commissioning editor. You may be asked to rewrite all or part of it.
To make a documentary: Work out the beginning, middle and end. Divide into distinct chapters e.g. 5 stories in a 15 minute film. Get light and shade and bring in some humour. (The donor of these tips was making a film about Mrs Thatcher who made much of being domesticated. So the directors suggested that she might make a cup of tea. Mrs T opened one cupboard – jams, another plates, a third pots and pans. It had become obvious that she had no idea about the kitchen but at last, relief – she spotted cups, saucers and Nescafé laid out and hastily said "Let's have coffee instead." Go for the unusual not the obvious; the quiet man may have more to say than the

loquacious one; someone who is struggling and winning through is always interesting. The editing is crucial so work closely with him/her.   10 minutes of rushes may make 1 minute of film. Give the editor a cutting order, make a rough cut and you hone it.

How to select a Play for Production *given by a former head of BBC writing and drama*
Spend three minutes reading the first and last three pages of the play and you will know if you have something worthwhile.

How to run a local Theatre *Explanation and tip given by a local theatre manager*
Local theatres are under serious threat of closure and are having to diversify into films and films of live performances but these are not necessarily easy options. If live theatre at local level stops, then talent will be missed and only the wealthy will be able to afford the training to go into the profession.
Be prepared to work a 70 hour week. Form a group of Friends who volunteer as ushers, etc. and get prior notification of programmes, etc. Ask people to "Be a Friend, bring a friend, buy a drink".

How to be a good Magician *given by an internationally known Master Magician*
Watch other Magicians. Watch Magicians on the internet via YouTube. Read magic books obtainable through many magic sites via Google. Join a Magic Society, ask a Magician for guidance and be yourself. Have Commitment, Self discipline, Patience, Communication and Dress for today's society. Enjoy entertaining others.

Medical

How to be a good Doctor *given by an expert retired GP and geriatrician*
Medicine used to be art backed by science but now it is becoming more science based and sadly much of the art is being lost.
Don't dress down or dress too informally. The doctor is a professional and the relationship is better if formality, though friendly, is maintained. Find out as much as you can about the patient before they come in. Always get up, shake hands, greet the patient by name and if it is a new or very confused patient introduce yourself.
Don't use patients' Christian names unless you are on very friendly terms. Listen and watch the patient. Don't bury yourself in the computer. For

intimate examinations make sure that privacy is maintained and explain what you are going to do.

Give clear instructions about drugs to be taken and what for and what further investigations or consultations will be needed. Give appropriate leaflet if necessary. Don't assume that they have taken in everything. Watch out for "By the way Doctor" scenario as the patient heads for the door; it may be the most important thing they say such as "By the way Doctor I have this pain in my chest or getting funny turns etc".

How to be a good Patient

Arrive on time and don't miss appointments.

For a GP remember that they can be very busy and he may be tired. Know or write down all the things you want to mention. Don't phone your GP however friendly in the middle of the night. Use emergency number given. A very busy GP was once woken in the middle of the night by a huge banging noise in the plumbing. He phoned the plumber who eventually replied saying "Put a couple of Paracetamol in the tank and ring me in the morning"

For a hospital appointment take your letter with you. Take a book with you and if new, a recent prescription sheet or all your medicines. Don't be afraid to take a friend with you and take notes. It is very easy to forget something that might be of vital importance.

When in hospital _always_ say if you don't understand something. Always tell a staff member if you feel things aren't going well. Make sure that your family talk to each other to avoid separate calls.

How to be a good Nurse

Care for your patients as you would wish your mother to be treated. Remember that people have had their own life before coming into hospital. Be kind to your team.

How to be a good Occupational Therapist

Be empathetic and build a rapport with the client. Respect his/her wishes. Have a 'can-do' attitude.

How to be a good Paramedic

Be caring. Listen to the patient and read between the lines e.g. patient may say that he is diabetic and asthmatic denying all else but later will say "After I had my heart attack". Keep your head. Be prepared for serious injuries and grisly fatalities. Keep a sense of humour.

How to be a good Speech Therapist
Be empathetic and build a rapport with the client. Respect his/her wishes. Be hard-working and non-judgemental. Have a "can do" attitude. *See also the tip on making labial sounds under "Health/Disability"*

How to be a good Dentist
Be a people person, communicate well and have patience. Get to know the patient. Explain what you are going to do and why and repeat this after a while. Keep up to date.

How to be a good Dental Patient
Attend regularly to establish a good rapport. Give a decent history, ie say what and where the problem is and when it started. Understand the problem and take ownership of it. <u>You</u> are responsible! Children should attend when really young – before any trouble starts.

How to be a good Vet *given by a senior partner in a busy Veterinary Practice*
Vets are "in practice" when they work. 'Practice makes perfect' but this is continuous – there is always something more to learn. Common things occur commonly (and less common things occur too). Always work towards achieving the outcome that is in the animal's best interests. It is never worth getting cross or impatient – animals always detect this and will bring you down to earth with a bump, a kick or a bite.

How to be a helpful Vet Customer
Give the vet the best possible opportunity to learn whatever they can about your pet – a full and relevant clinical history. Be calm and give your pet the best opportunity to be calm himself.
Be aware that veterinary medicine and surgery can be offered at many different levels – from the high technology of CT and MRI scanning, laparoscopic surgery, spinal surgery, etc through general surgery, blood tests to antibiotics and pain relief – so, decide with your vet what is needed for your pet.

Music
How to be a good Brass Band team member *given by a band saxophonist*
Do what the leader says. Take your instrument to bits occasionally to clean and oil with 3-in-1 Oil.

How to start and run a Music Society *from a successful Music Society founder*
Join the national federation Making Music which gives advice on performing rights, insurance, performers and insurance. Allow for performers fees, travel expenses and hospitality, etc. Churches make good venues because of their ambience, space, acoustics and organs (if good) but heating, lighting and hard pews may pose problems. Pianos are problematic. It's best to hire one if required.

Plan a varied programme of right length (not more than 2 hours including an interval). Form links with local schools. Performers often like to visit schools and grants may be available.

How to be a good Orchestral Soloist *given by a Professor of Cello*
You need good stamina, excellent hearing (as well as perfect pitch) to pick up the orchestra behind and communicate with them. For concerts leave plenty of preparation time and pace yourself.

How to be a good Organist *given by a Committee Member of the Royal Society of Organists*
Love and understand music. Get well trained. Listen to other organists . *(It is possible to do a conversion course from piano to organ.)*

Police and Fire

How to be a good Police Officer *given by a former head of the Ashford Police Training School and an Acting Chief Constable*
Sir John Peel said that the Constabulary was created for the prevention and detection of crime and the maintenance of law and order. Get to know your area and people and ignore stupid and rude remarks. Have a responsible attitude, honesty, courtesy, integrity, confidence, tolerance and social awareness. Be able to assess a situation, react quickly, take positive action and stay calm in sometimes life threatening situations. Have courage, initiative and common sense, strong communication skills and knowledge of the Law.

How to help the Police
Be available when appointments are made or phone response is requested. Be cooperative in helping the police to reduce crime. Don't label all officers as similar. Each is different and one bad experience shouldn't apply to all. Have realistic expectations. Police powers are limited by the information

given to them. Give the information you deem relevant. One fact may be vital. Keep accurate records of ongoing concerns. Feed this back and notify any changes. Report any grave concerns about neighbours or colleagues. Be aware that justice is not always achieved despite much investigation. Start or join a Neighbourhood Watch scheme.

How to be a good On-Call Fire Officer *given by a veteran Fire Officer*
You need to be brave and physically fit. A good team spirit, enthusiasm and commitment to serve your community are essential. Live within 5 mins (walking or driving) from the station. Be available on weekdays during the daytime and weekends. (Full-time is not advised)

How the Public can help the Fire Service
Although the Fire Service has specialist teams to rescue large domestic animals, you should contact the owner/farmer first.
Farmers do usually protect their animals against mishaps.
For smaller animals contact the RSPCA.

Shopping
How to be a good Shopkeeper
Be extra kind to the elderly. Listen to the customers and have a genuine concern for their needs. Treat them as you would like to be treated. Have pride in keeping high standards and reliability. Be patient: bespoke and complex items take time to source *(being patient, kind and friendly with customers is a sine qua non). Remember that 'the shopkeeper' forms the backbone of our country – Margaret Thatcher.*
An elderly and very confused gentleman used to go into a well-known store, fill his trolley, walk straight through the till without paying, put everything in the car and drive off. At the end of each week his daughter would go to the customer services desk where she would be told "These are the bills for your father – Monday, Wednesday and Friday, etc." and she would pay the final tally putting something in the charity box as she left.

How to be a good Independent Supermarket Owner
Work hard all hours, Monday to Sunday, and keep fit – you walk for miles around a shop. Talk and listen to customers. Have good IT, financial and organisational skills; also good interpersonal skills to manage and recruit staff. Have an eye for something different and keep abreast of the market. Retail is constantly changing. Know when to say no.

How to be a good Marketer
Know your product and be able to demonstrate how to use it.
How to be a good Shop Attendant or Volunteer Helper:
Remember the three S's – Smile. Be smart. Be secure.
How to be a good customer
Know what you want. Be friendly and honest with the staff and give constructive criticism if appropriate. Talk to them and develop mutual respect.
How to be a good Customer Service Team member
Put yourself in the other person's shoes. Remember that perceptions of politeness change e.g. for younger people it is acceptable to answer a mobile phone while talking to someone else.

How to be a good Diplomat *given by a retired Ambassador*
In one word, "Listen."
(On the other hand Sir Henry Wotton 1568 – 1639 said that "An ambassador is an honest man sent to lie for his country.")
How to be a good Inventive Designer *given by a brilliant inventor who invented among other things a drone to monitor railway lines to protect them from theft*
Use every spare moment to think of inventive ideas. Always keep a notebook and pen with you to sketch ideas and jot them down. Original thoughts sometimes come in dreams – keep paper and pen by your bed.
Acquire useful skills such as CAD (computer aided design) and CAM (computer aided manufacturing). Best invention may solve many problems at a time e.g. finding an application for an abundant waste product (e.g. a charity Practical Action found that impacting coir dust in India could make burnable fire bricks).
Drop any idea at once if you or others find it flawed. List essential qualities such as the likeness, cost, etc., before embarking. Ask questions however simple; often others are wondering about the same thing. When costing an idea consider anything needed to get it to the user – manufacture, marketing, packaging, warehouse delivery etc. Cheap is not always best.
Pick the brains of relatives and friends for ideas. Check ideas with a reliable mentor before committing time and money to them. Be prepared to license them to larger organisations with the clout to protect and market them. Don't let brilliant ideas fail because of poor preparation and presentation.

How to be a good Librarian
Be a people person. Have a conversation – assess what the user wants and ask questions if necessary. Be organised, patient and have a sense of curiosity and humour.

How to use a library *given by a librarian but not the official judgements of the library*
When asking for a book, giving the title and author is better than the ISBN number which can cause confusion. Be aware that librarians give advice on many subjects and that libraries have many facilities including having computers available with free wifi and internet connections as well as talking books etc. Ask the question you want the answer to, not the question you think the librarian can answer. Ask what is available e.g. free reference sources such as Ancestry online and free loans of e-books. Make sure you know your card and pin number – so that you can reserve and renew titles online or by phone. Ask for advice and learn how to search the catalogue e.g. for Somerset, somerset.gov.uk/libraries. Libraries have Talking Books, DVDs, Music on CDs and large print books. They give advice on many topics e.g. contact numbers of voluntary organisations such as RNIB: Benefits, Jobs and using the web. Wifi and prolonged use of computers is now free.

How to be a good Lifeboat Crew Member *given by a long serving volunteer who has the O.B.E.*
You need bravery, commitment and availability (living within one mile of the boat), unselfishness and family support.

How to be a good Magistrate
Have an open mind. Do not judge a book by its cover.

How to be a good Post Office Manager
Be patient and helpful and have a friendly relationship with staff and the public. Be able to work under pressure at difficult times and be prepared for a hold-up. Look after the property or report faults to landlord. Act as a shopkeeper either with stationery or as a general store. This attracts more customers. Understand the 200 transactions carried out including travel, home and car insurance; implement a range of investments; arrange a range of Royal Mail transactions; act as a bureau de change; deal with pensions and family allowance; sell lottery tickets; check photographs and passport and driving licence applications.

How to be a helpful Post Office customer: Know the correct address and postcode of mail. Be aware of the numerous services offered including the facility to bank and withdraw money with UK banks.
Put an address label on the back of mail to help Royal Mail and don't cancel all your junk mail, it is a large source of income for the post office. Don't come to the desk with unwrapped parcels. *(Yes, it happens. To date no one has been lynched by an angry queue.)* If travelling abroad you can't necessarily trust all officials. When in India the editor was given far too little cash in a post office exchange. When questioned the clerk quickly pulled a large note from under the counter with "I was about to give you this."
How to be a good Potter *given by a master potter, grandson of Bernard Leach CBE founder of the St Ives Pottery.* His pots, which excel in beauty and usefulness can be obtained in Muchelney, Somerset
www.johnleachpottery.co.uk / 01458 250324. Try his wonderful casseroles and fridge jugs.
Throwing a pot on the potter's wheel is a wonderfully sensual, meditative and therapeutic process. It is hypnotic, peaceful and very satisfying. You need (i) an innate feel and understanding of the raw material, clay, and what is technically possible to achieve good results; (ii) a practical approach to the craft exercising diligence, perseverance, humility and a willingness to learn skills and techniques from a master potter; (iii) some knowledge of the history of pot making in other countries, giving inspiration and a wide perspective that one can always tap into; and (iv) selling, marketing experience and good business acumen.
How to be a good Prison Officer *given by a former Chief Inspector of Prisons*
You need: The ability to create good working relationships with people from all walks of life with an open mind and the ability to act fairly in disputes besides patience, understanding and a commitment to helping people.
You also need the ability to work in a structured environment where rules and discipline apply, the ability to stay calm, assess a situation, make quick decisions and to cope with pressure.
Have good team working skills, a firm but fair approach and exercise authority with abusive or possibly violent prisoners.
How to be a good Publisher *given by the Head of a large London publishing house and a former Publisher who ran his own publishing house*
"I object to publishers. The one thing they have taught me is to do without them. They combine commercial rascality with artistic pettiness, being

neither fine judges of literature nor good businessmen." **George Bernard Shaw**

A publisher is paid to exercise judgement with an inner intuitive sense. Is it good? Is it worth publishing? Never ask sales people for an opinion. They want everything to be like something else they know e.g. just to publish bestsellers.

Don't go for outsiders' blurbs e.g. Prince Charles says . . . this is wonderful." Rely on yourself and don't blame others if things do not work out. Pick authors with a flair for self publicity. No one will be as familiar with the book as they are.

The computer has given authors verbal diarrhoea. The best books are sparing and economic. They are best written by hand on a lined pad. Follow St Benedict and read slowly. Take the words from the eyes into the mind and then absorb them into the heart.

"The trouble with modern men and women is that they have cocktail parties going on inside their heads." **Martin Laird** *Into the Silent Land*

Be prepared to work hard and to read fast by scanning down the centre of the page. Many manuscripts will arrive and though many can be rejected after reading only a few pages, others will need to be read right through. Attend the major book fairs but most clients are found by word of mouth. The days of meeting clients for a good lunch are over but allow enough time for coffee. Having a second or third language is a great asset.

How to be a good racehorse trainer *given by a Somerset trainer*

Most trainers learn the art as an assistant. Be able to communicate well with owners. Get on well with your staff and have a happy team and a good routine: the horses' performance will reflect the happiness of the team. Source horses at the right price for the owners and go through a bloodstock agent as to travel to Ireland or France takes time and money. Be able to run a business and lastly able to train the horses and place them in the right races. An old adage is "Trainers should be in the best company and horses in the worst."

Betting at the races: 'The Race is not always to the swift, nor the fight to the strong but that's the way to bet.' Never place a bet with a bookie who smokes a large cigar or has an expensive car.

How to be a good British Horse Racing Steward

You need total integrity, full knowledge of racing plus fairness and consistency of judgement.

How to be a good Restaurateur *given by an excellent Thai restaurateur in Langport and another excellent one in Curry Rivel*
Be prepared to work very hard. Start small and aim to build with something modest and easily handled. Know your market and offer great food and value for money.
Watch expenditure. Offering best quality ingredients and keeping prices down is difficult but can be done. Constantly try to do better. Don't even start if you haven't got a sense of humour.
Employ excellent staff. Create a home from home ambiance for your guests. Have best quality fresh ingredients and excellent homemade food made from scratch.
How to be a good Secretary *given by a retired secretary who worked among other places with the Duke of Edinburgh's Award and the International Antique Dealers' Show*
Smile, be punctual and polite, particularly to juniors and dress smartly. Do unspecified tasks, including making the office tea and coffee. Use good telephone manners, mentioning the name of your organisation. Implement instructions from your boss quickly and keep a diary for him and yourself including family names and birthdays. Make sure letters do not have spelling and grammar errors – a boss does not like correcting typing mistakes. When taking minutes have all necessary information needed for the meeting and anticipate questions that may require your knowledge. Use your initiative.
How to be a good Taxi Driver *given by a town and a London Cabby*
Be respectful, helpful, friendly and well insured. Get clients safely to their destination. Take the necessary examinations on locations – these last over a two year period; also the additional driving tests. Get to the speed limit allowed as fast and smoothly as possible. Never argue. Beware of trouble at night. If you see someone drunk or dressed in a smart but dishevelled way, don't stop.   If you have stopped, quote an exorbitant price. They may wait for another cab. If they accept, ask for advanced payment. Agree with everything said. If they won't pay let them go. A broken window costs more than the fare.
If you want the London black cab to survive, don't use the Uber mini-cabs which have an oval green sticker in the rear window. They are supposed to give a fixed price before starting the journey but use a mobile phone as a meter to judge distance and time which can't be easily verified.

They cause extra congestion as they outnumber black cabs, do not know London well and often take the wrong lane etc. Moreover they are based in Holland thus avoiding U.K. tax.

How to be a good Trucker

A trucker should be prepared to work long spells away from home and be able to change their sleep pattern. Some knowledge of other languages is useful but much less so with the advent of Sat Nav. Do not trust any car driver as they do not know how a truck operates. Advice for car drivers and cyclists: the rigid truck, coaches and buses need a large arc to turn around so give them lots of space. The articulated (artic) truck can turn in a very small arc and when in a car or on a bike in the inside lane when he is turning left the truck driver cannot see you. This is one of the most frequent causes of road deaths despite signs on the truck saying "If you can't see my mirrors, I can't see you". A right turn is safer but still causes accidents.

(The rules for a trucker are complicated. He must comply with the general working time directive law that for every 6 hours worked there must be a 30 minute break.   This runs in parallel with the European drivers' rules and regulations for truckers and coach drivers. They can work for 5 hours twice a week: after 4½ hours' driving they must have a 45 minute break – for refinement refer to Internet. The tachograph recording of a driver's schedule is inspected by VOSA (Vehicle Operation Standards Authority). The exams start with 7 ½ ton vehicles, then Class 2 rigid trucks up to 26 tons, then Class 1 articulated trucks up to 44 tons.)

HUMOUR

Sense of humour
It is useful to know that this varies with nationality. e.g., the **Japanese** find it excruciatingly funny if seven men jump out of the plane and six of the parachutes fail to open. The **Irish** enjoy a long story ending in the Irish Giant (Fin McCoull) getting the better of all comers especially the English or Scottish or the underdog doing likewise to someone in authority. The **Americans** like to make jokes as the situation arises. e.g. Groucho Marks (1890-1977) when told to have a 'nice day' replied 'thanks but I have other plans'.
The **Swedish** are a bit humourless but like the English/Irish they have Swedish/Norwegian jokes, such as "Why do Norwegians drive with windscreen wipers on the inside? – Because of all the spitting as they go Brrrrm, brrrrm, brrrrrrrrrrm.
The **French** joke relies heavily on black humour and tends to be very cruel and disgusting. Nothing is considered too close to the bone. The editor was given one based on the Germans' maltreatment of Jews which was too distasteful to print. They also enjoy spoonerisms, all of which are too filthy to print! They have better jokes, mocking the Belgians e.g. "Why do Belgian dogs have flat noses?" "Because they chase after parked cars." Occasionally the jokes are about themselves. E.g. De Gaulle is reputed to have said, "How can anyone govern a country that has 360 kinds of cheese?" or "Why do the French have straight roads?" "To make it easier for the Germans to invade them."

The general gist is that it's funny if it offends someone. Otherwise, there is a long tradition of wordplay and puns. The English don't really understand the French – one broadcaster said "The trouble with the French is that they don't know the meaning of the word 'sang froid'."

German humour is varied: one young French student who had spent time in a German senior school said that German humour tends to be scatological but try these.

"Did you perhaps leave your wife because she now wears glasses?" Siggy asks a friend. "No, she left me when she got her glasses."
"Fritz, did your divorce go through quickly?" "Yes, we even had to cut short our honeymoon."
"Mum, what's a werewolf?" "Be quiet and comb your face."

Italians like to laugh at politicians and situations and to make puns. Berlusconi is in a helicopter and says, "I'll throw €10 out of the window and make one Italian happy." Later he says "I'll throw €20 out of the window and make 2 Italians happy. A passenger then rejoins, "Why not throw yourself out and make all Italians happy?"

Spaniards like to see themselves as smart compared to other nationalities, especially their North African neighbours. A Spanish gypsy has the reputation for being the smartest and the term is not derogatory: A Gypsy and a Moor go into a bakery. The Moor steals a cake, puts it in his pocket and asks the Gypsy, "Did you see the artist?" The Gypsy answers "We'll see who's the better artist!" The baker comes in and the Gypsy says "Give me a cake and I'll show you some magic." The baker is intrigued and gives him the cake whereupon the Gypsy eats it and looks the baker long and hard straight in the eyes. The baker is not amused and asks the Gypsy, "Where is the magic in that?". The Gypsy says, "Look in the Moor's trouser pocket."

There are jokes at the expense of other regions. Catalans are seen as stingy like the English view of the Scots: How do you get 10 Catalans in a taxi? Tell them there is a 5 pence coin inside. How do you get them out again quickly? Tell them it's a taxi.

They like to laugh at civil servants or other professions. This comes from the days when the civil service day would start (theoretically) at 8am and finish at 2pm: A man visits a government office and asks the doorman if he can see a certain official and is told the man is not there. "What?" he says, "Don't they work in the afternoons?" "You've got it all wrong" says the doorman. "When they don't work is in the mornings. They don't come in the afternoons." The **Chinese** rarely make jokes because they hate loosing face or causing others to do so – but try this. A small boy was found alone and crying in a

large department store. They ask, "What's the matter?" "I have lost my Mum." "What's she like?" "Shopping and gossiping."
A **Nigerian** friend of the editor gave as an example, "A dwarf kicking a calabash."
English: Cockney relies on instant wit. The editor once asked a barrow boy about his Russian matches. "Do they work?" His instant reply was, "Of course, every one has been tested."
Humour may be **inadvertent,** such as Ian Duncan-Smith's comment "The government has ruined our Public Health Services – Health, Education and Crime."
Sarcasm may be the lowest form of wit but has its place. A famous physician was asked for a reference by a junior doctor and wrote, "Dr X tells me he has worked for me." He also said "When another young doctor, visiting his house, knocked a priceless Ming vase off its stand and apologised profusely, he said, 'Never mind. It was very old'."
Puns may be the next lowest form of wit but were used effectively by Thomas Hood (1799-1845) in the poem 'Faithless Sally Brown' as a double pun:
>His death which happened in his birth *(berth)*
>At 40 odd befell.
>They went and told the sexton.
>The sexton tolled the bell.

The pun 'As she wrings her ring-less hands' is used by many writers including Fanny Hurst, Lawrence Durrell and Mills and Boon. Shakespeare's puns are mostly too bawdy to print but Prospero says 'Admirable Miranda indeed the top of admirable' - a pun on the Latin mirare - to admire.

Humour Faux Pas
Faux pas are easy to make. In America take care. For a man saying, "I'll call you" or "I'll call you up" is extremely rude as it implies that the lady is a prostitute.
They are easy to make in other languages too. A general wanted to thank the Russian band musicians (moozicant) but in fact thanked the "moozhic" (peasant). A businessman in Russia had the opening words of his speech written in Russian but realised that "Ladies and Gentlemen" was not included. He spotted a sign for the toilets and inserted the words written there. Unfortunately on this occasion the Russian for "Gentlemen" was given as "urinals". A minor diplomat visiting the French county town of Eu did not

realise that the local people are extremely careful to refer to him as "Le maire de la cité d'Eu".

In New Zealand, if someone says to you "You have bowled underhand" or "That was an underhander." It implies that you cheated or played foul.

Faux pas are easily made in Chinese as intonation is all important e.g. the word "ma" has 5 different meanings including mother and horse so it is possible but inadvisable to say, "You look just like your horse" rather than "mother".

MOVING HOUSE

Remember that moving house, especially to a new area, is stressful, second only to bereavement and divorce in one's life. Move to an area close to friends, join a club, take on some charity work and find the right church for you if you are a church goer. It is much easier to make friends if your children are at a local school. Research schools well in advance.

Look in the winter, sell in the spring. Never believe all the house agents say. Three months in advance of moving, clear the attic, sort the garage and garden shed. Give unwanted things to your family or charity shop. Plan any building or redecoration work needed. Book the move with a recommended removals firm. One month in advance, select, label and pot up wanted plants. Get various colour and shape sticky labels to show the final room selected. Select a new school. Send change of address cards. Get maps of the new area. Make a plan to scale of each room on graph paper and cut out and label pieces of paper with to scale furniture items and floor rugs. Juggle to fit as you wish then draw them in the plan. You will then be able to tell the removal men exactly where items are to go. Windows can similarly be measured for curtains.

Make sure house is insured from date of purchase.

Have a kettle, snacks, mugs, tea, coffee, sugar and whisky immediately available on arrival. Book your family into a nearby hotel for two nights if needed. Order flowers or a pot plant to be delivered to the house on arrival but remember to have a vase or saucer ready.

When established dial 101 and ask a Police Community Support Officer for tips on burglary protection. They will visit and will notice things that you don't.

If moving to a new military married quarter, get a list of local knowledge from the previous regiment. (During the height of the IRA troubles in Northern Ireland, a regiment in Omagh which, at the time, was a friendly town, told the butcher how to recognise their new intelligence officer. He was dismayed when going into the butcher in mufti the butcher looked at him and said, "Oh, you must be the new spy, Sir.")

Moving with children
Visit the new home, area and school when possible. Move their room first and keep in a similar layout to your previous home. Let them choose decor, etc.

House security from crime
Vital points: Pale noisy gravel is safer than a smooth surface surrounding the house. Keep the garage doors locked. Keys should not be visible or near any door or window. Windows – Double glazing is safer than single, secure locks are needed. Doors need mortise as well as Yale locks – the latter are easily opened with a credit card.
Hiding valuables. A burglar will search the bedroom drawers first, spare cash (notes) can be hidden in a book.
For fire safety advice (particularly important if there are frail elderly or young children in the house) if in Devon or Somerset phone Devon and Somerset Fire and Rescue Service on 01823 365365 (the number given in present phone directory is false) and ask for Fire and Safety Advice. An advocate will give immediate advice and will arrange a home visit if necessary.

Moving abroad
Get any foreign electric plugs necessary, also universal rubber plugs for plumbing. Stock up on batteries. Make language cards of common words for all the family.
If moving to Florida check the walls for termites. They may collapse if termites are active. This may also apply in the Far East.

Buildings *from a master builder*
Your house is your biggest investment. Take time to look after it.

Maintenance
Most problems are caused by water. Act before it is a crisis.
Keep waste traps in sinks, baths etc clear of debris e.g. hair, vegetable matter, oils and fat, which congeal, blocking them. Replace taking care not to cross the thread. If one tap in a room drips replace all the washers on the taps as they are the same age. Check the locality of the mains water stop cock annually, that it works and isn't obstructed. In the Autumn after leaf fall clear gutters, down pipes and gullies of leaves/debris. Check all joints are tight. Check overflows from roof tank and WCs. If they are dripping or running replace ball valve. Act before disaster! Check walls that paths, soil etc. do not cover the damp-proof course causing rising damp, and check for flaking paint or plaster. (Dry rot smells of mushrooms – act fast).

Major building works
Choose contractors carefully. Ask for recommendations. Are any similar jobs being done locally? Consult the owners. Research costs little, lack of it could cost you sanity. Get ball park estimates – a full quote may cost a great deal. Have a meeting of an hour or so to talk it over. Have a plan and stick to it. Changes later may cost a lot. Get a formal quote and terms. Don't choose just on price.

Don't pay up front – reputable professionals aren't paying up front for materials. Make staged payments when work is satisfactorily completed.
Building a Zero Energy (Passive) House *given by a savvy retired vet in Omagh, co Tyrone).*
For under floor heating, heat ground and upper floors if possible. Use a ground source heat pump if the ground is damp clay or boggy (it is the rain which carries the heat in more than the sun). If the ground is fast draining sand or gravel use an air source pump. Use solar panels to heat the water. Shop around for the most efficient type. For power, use photovoltaic panels. Get the tariff for feeding power into the grid but install a system that will divert the power to heat water if sun not hot enough. Power from PVE panels will be reduced by 50% if any one panel is in shade therefore install a system that will cut out the shaded panels leaving the rest to run at 100%. Use double or triple glazing. Use adequate fibre glass insulation (400mm thick in roof) and recommended type and thickness of insulation in walls which vary a lot.

PETS

Dog fouling indoors: Don't use bleach as it smells like excrement. Keep a bag of sawdust handy for when your dog does a poo on a hard surface. Sprinkle liberally and leave for 10-15 minutes then shovel it up. Sweep up any excess sawdust.

For a young dog who reverts to fouling, don't chastise, ignore it. It may be seeking attention. Don't let him see you cleaning up.

To remove cat's pee odour, clean the surface with bio detergent then with surgical spirit or gin or try white vinegar alone or after bio detergent.

If your dog jumps up, grasp a paw and hold it up but don't try with stray dogs. Bend down to talk to pets.

To get a dog to let go of something in its mouth, press the side of its lip hard against its upper teeth. It will soon let go.

RELATIONSHIPS

Family Dynamics
Remember that Christmas is stressful because the many different age groups have different needs.

Marriage
A recipe for a good marriage: Stand up to the world back to back. Picture an old master painting that you love. Think of the artist having a large pot of turpentine to soften hardened oils which he keeps on a top shelf in his studio. Think of God's grace as like that pot of turpentine and reach up to the top shelf and bring it down whenever the situation needs softening *(from a wedding sermon preached by an elderly minister for his granddaughter's wedding).* Take your spouse on a long drive without others.

Marital discord: If things are going badly wrong arrange a time to yourselves to talk calmly through the issues and see other's difficulties. Consult a trusted friend, priest or minister. Marriage guidance is helpful but they do not give advice. Try to see each other's needs and what you can each do to make things better. When discussing things and overcoming anger, breathe in counting one, two, three, and out counting one, two, three. As you breathe in, say to yourself "in with the anger" and as you breathe out "out with the love". It is thought by many that stress can lead to cancer but this is not proven. Say "You could" not "You should" "never go to bed on a row".

Arguments: Instead of "You said x y z", try "I find it difficult when we quarrel about x y z.". Remember that anger can increase the risk of heart disease. There are books on managing anger. Conciliare aut caedare (conciliate or kill) is a useful maxim for bringing matters to a head but the best cure for anger and flying off the handle is delay. A friend once told me that the sex drive is "like being manacled to a maniac".

Children need to express anger in a safe environment but they need to know the boundaries. Try to talk them through their anger. Never issue a threat that you are not prepared to follow up e.g. if you threaten to confiscate the computer you must do so if the situation arises, but as Oliver Cromwell said "Be prepared to admit that you are wrong".

If you have found a long lost relative via the internet or other method, invite them to your house first not vice versa. If done the wrong way the relative may feel intimidated and not wish to continue with the new relationship. (This is even more important with children.)

Prayers
If you want to pray for sick friends put their names on the stairs.

Christmas
Christmas cards: Some people are sending email messages and giving the money saved to charity but the preference is for a real card. A short message enhances the value of the card. Put a name and address sticker on the card (or on the back of the envelope) - saves embarrassment when faced with "Love from John (who?)" or "Jack and Gill (who?)", especially for the elderly.

Christmas presents
Keep lists of to whom sent and from whom received each year. Buy presents early (e.g. when on holiday). Keep a store for adults, children and babies in a drawer. Ask parents what a child wants/needs.

Teenagers
When teenagers go away on holiday, instead of being miserable strip the bed and put on clean linen immediately.

Young children
Rearing young children: As well as keeping a baby book and photos, make a note of some of their sayings to you and to others.
Entertaining young children: A square of old net curtain will give hours of entertainment for a young girl and is light to pack. "Spookyspecial" or other boxed face painting kits will delight a wide age range of children. Involve them in general jobs such as cooking, gardening and washing cars. The task will take longer and make more mess but they will enjoy it.
If you have your weekly shopping delivered to your home, time it so that they can help unpack it. It takes longer but they love it. Pack valuable or

breakable things separately. Keep any boxes delivered to the house. Children love pretending they are trains, houses or just hiding in them and jumping out saying "Boo!".

Make a magic bag – an old shopping or handbag that you can put lots of things in for the children to unpack and play with; e.g. bubble wrap, cardboard tubes, homemade shakers, postcards, make up or anything they love to play with, but not their own toys. It will make the place untidy but can be packed up at the end of the day. A square of old net curtain will give hours of entertainment for a young girl and is light to pack.

Enjoy time in the bath. Play with bubbles in the bath - refilling with Fairy Liquid suitably diluted. Get little capsules made by Tec UK called "Growing sea life creatures" which grow in water. Teach boys never to hit a girl with anything stronger than a flower.

Young families

Prenatal help: If possible offer used prams, clothes, etc. as a gift or loan. For a postnatal mum who is struggling, call round with flowers or ready made food. Offer to take laundry home, do shopping, etc. Later on, offer to lend or hand on used clothes, good toys or baby equipment. Later still offer to hand on school uniform or to share school runs.

Looking after friends

Keeping in contact is paramount. Don't be afraid to phone if a friend is bereaved. They may want and need to talk to a friend about their loss and to hear about the wonderful qualities their loved one had. If you are nearby, take some flowers or suitable food.

SPEAKING AND WRITING SKILLS

Writing
When writing poetry, prose, a talk or instructions, cut out all the superfluous adjectives. (This is particularly important for poetry.) Do not use a long complicated word where a short Anglo-Saxon one will do. It is much more punchy. This is advice given by Seamus Heaney and the late poet laureate Ted Hughes. For a poem draft and re-draft, making it as short as possible. Keep adjectives and exclamations marks to a minimum.

Writing Letters
When writing a letter, address the envelope first. *(as per Lewis Carrol).*

Writing a Biography *given by a distinguished biographer*
Don't do it unless you are really keen on your subject as it takes time to research and write a biography – it's like a marriage. Before you commit yourself find out if there is enough interesting material available. You can't make bricks without straw. Check what has already been written about your subject and be sure that you have something substantial or new to contribute. Research is infinitely expandable and seductive. Make a date for when you will start writing and stick to it, even if you still have things to find out. Enjoy your work. Life-writing is inexhaustible, absorbing and satisfying.

Writing Poetry *by James Crowden, a Somerset poet*

>Writing poetry?
>There's a difficult one.
>You see the words do not always
>Go to the end of the line.
>
>The line can be a fishing line
>And you wait till the muse nibbles.
>The thoughts arise
>Like bubbles or trout
>And then, in a clear moment,
>Out pops the poem.

But it's not quite as easy as it looks
And sometimes poems
Are hung out to dry on hooks
And some, just a few, may
Even end up in books.

Preaching a Sermon
Sermons should be like bikinis: brief and covering all the vital points. They should be short and have one clear point to take away and ponder. "Thought for the Day", at about 7:50 am on BBC Radio 4, takes 3 minutes; but short sermons are more difficult to write than long ones.

Public Speaking *given by a well known successful parliamentarian.*
To make a speech at a party conference (or any other large gathering), write the opening and closing sentences on a card – you can also write heading of subject to come between and names. This avoids doing an Ed Milliband voice drop at the end of a sentence becoming inaudible and losing the meaning or punchline.

SPORT

Cricket
Facing a demon bowler *(given by Geoff Boycott while commentating)* "The way to deal with that demon spinbowling of Shane Warne is to take a quick single and let your partner take the flack" *(or was it to watch him from the other end?).*

Hockey
Get kit ready the night before. Take a plastic bag for muddy boots. Don't put any deep heat ointment (good for aching muscles) in your jock strap and don't do it to anyone else either.

Riding
If you fall off, remount as soon as possible. If you think anything to do with horses is only going to take 10 mins allow an hour. If you think it will take all day it may only take 10 mins.
After riding or watching someone riding or playing any other type of game in the cold, especially a school outside sport, have a flask ready containing hot Bovril and port in 3:1 proportion heated to near boiling point. This revives like nothing else, but get someone else to drive!
Advanced riding: If practising jumping, first of all do some basic control: walk, stop, walk, stop, etc for 45 minutes. The horse will jump much better. Good dressage is the key to good jumping.
How to get a boy to ride: Do all the stable work, care of the fields, grooming and tacking up yourself. Take the pony to the mounting block and he will have a hell of a time of reckless hunting. You then only have to do all the pony care, clean the tack and launder his clothes.

Rugby *given by a former school Rugby coach who played for the Welsh under 21's)*
Be 100% fit. Learn the skills of kicking with left and right foot, passing to left and right, the scissors and dummy moves, the long kick to the corner and the Garry Owen (the ball goes high over the opponents head). Get the wings to come in on the blind side. i.e., between the scrum and the line for a possible try. Remember that a try can be made by touching the ball on the line or the

base of the goalpost as well as behind the line. Practice penalty and drop kicks. A coach known to him would say 'get your retaliation in first lads' but learn safe tackling and safety in the scrum and don't be a fairy tackler. Avoid head crashing and choke tackling. Brain damage has increased in rugby recently. Recognise the signs of serious injury and call the ref at once. Don't indulge in 'hand bagging'. In the scrum, if your hooker gets the ball from the opposition's throw in, this is 'one against the head' - a useful expression if you managed to get a drink out of Mr Miser.

Sailing   *told to the editor by a European Royal Olympic Gold winner in the1960 Olympics.*
Racing at sea: Keep looking up and watch every ripple caused by the wind. In England the tide is everything so consult local knowledge and the tide charts before setting out. Place yourself where the tide is and watch other boats to see if they are picking up tide or wind. Keep the hull clear of barnacles. In UK boats over 65' are not allowed to use antifouling paint (and yet much larger boats and ships are allowed to.) Scrub the hull every two weeks.
Racing on lakes: this is predominant in Europe. The wind is all important and can change rapidly especially if close to mountains. Again, consult local knowledge, watch other boats and keep the hull clean. Weed is more likely to come from some rivers than others.
Sea sickness: Stay outside warm, dry and occupied. If going below get flat as soon as possible. Vomit or pee on the leeward (downwind) side.

How to be a good Surfer
Learn to swim and practise hard in a pool. Understand how a wave and a surfboard work. (Waves are formed far out at sea. They coalesce to form the swell that we see rolling over and getting higher as they reach the beach.) The board is multi-layered with slightly curved edges so that, as with the ski, it will turn. (These are simplified explanations.)

Tennis
Be balanced on your feet. To keep fit, play singles. You also improve your play by playing singles as you have to be accurate in a confined space. Use the edges and the bottom corners of the court. Keep your opponent on the

run. When serving to the left hand court look at the net post on the right hand side and your ball will land in the correct area.
A curious rule: If you are standing behind the court and you catch the ball which is obviously going out, it is the opponent's point.
It is pointless getting angry and throwing your racket out of the court. There are no fairies and you will have to get it yourself.

Water Safety
Swimming in the sea: *Official lifeguard tips.*
Basic safety: Swim at a life guarded beach and between yellow and red flags. Never use inflatables in strong winds or rough seas. If you get into trouble try to stay calm, stick your hand in the air and shout for help.
If you see someone in trouble notify the lifeguard; if none are present, dial 999 or 112 and ask for lifeguard.
If you find yourself in a rip current: Stay calm. Raise your hand and shout for help. Never swim against the rip. Try to swim parallel to the shore until free of rip then swim to shore.
If you swallow a lot of water or hit your head, seek medical advice.

TRAVEL AND HOLIDAYS

Travel
Before leaving the house, to deter burglary, save energy and guard against fire, close the blinds, turn off appliances, make sure that windows and external doors and windows are closed and that the alarm is set. Set up a time switch for a lamp and, if possible, a recording of domestic noises.
If you can't afford the insurance, don't go. If you are going to a trouble spot country only go if you have to.

Packing
Make a tick off list of necessities. Put all the clothes out on a bed and decide which to take then halve the clothes and double the money. On return, add to your pared down list the things that were required and keep for future use. Pack the edge of the suitcase and the centre will pack itself. Take a length of nylon string to act as a clothes line.
Keep a small sewing kit (as provided in better hotels – they usually advertise the hotel) in suitcase together with a small tube of UHU or Bostic and back up drugs if you are on essential regular drugs. It can take at least 48 hours to replenish from your own pharmacy if have been left at home. For routine pharmacy it is better to buy abroad. Many drugs are cheaper in Europe than the UK. Get a local pharmacist to explain the instructions as the language may be a mystery.

Jet lag: After boarding the plane, drink some fluids. Don't take any alcohol. Take a short acting sleeping tablet and go straight to sleep. Melatonin may adjust the sleep pattern.

Mosquitos: A temporary shield can be made using an old net curtain on a string or spring wire to cover any open windows. Mosquito coils and plug in electric devices are obtainable at hardware shops.
Fly spray is better than a roll on spray. Use citronella or essence of lavender. Fire fighters in Arizona found that Avon moisturiser was a good deterrent. It is also good for New Zealand sand flies.
In a hot climate turn your boots and shoes upside down and give them a good shake in case you find a scorpion. It has been known . . .

Keep a packet of wet wipes or a small damp flannel in a plastic bag with you to wipe your face. When on an aircraft ask the air hostess if you can buy the small white hot flannel she brings to you. She will probably be happy to give it to you. They are ideal and hard to source.

If you are a frequent traveller by air, carry an emergency kit containing a silver foil blanket for cold or to catch dew in the desert; a fishing hook and line; a satellite phone and a mirror to flash sunlight to signal alert also a flat-formed Swiss army knife containing a penknife and scissors and a magnesium/flint fire starter. You strike the rod of magnesium containing a flint with the attached piece of steel over dry grass or other kindling (YouTube has good instructions.)

Take an empty bottle to the airport and fill it after passing security.

If a plane is delayed abroad and you are asked to get off it, refuse to budge until meals and a hotel are guaranteed – get others to do likewise.

To prevent loss of sunhat – cut the end off some old braces – as long as possible. Form a loop, glue with UHU or Evostick, and tape over that. Slip the loop over the waist belt and clip on the hat when not worn.

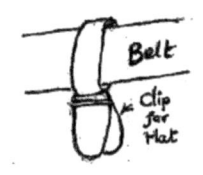

Opening up flimsy paper napkins. Tear one corner and you can see the layers.

Visiting France *given by a French Lady with immaculate manners*
When meeting someone always say "Bonjour" Madame, Monsieur or Mademoiselle or their Christian name if you know them and hold your hand out to shake theirs. Supermarket and shop attendants expect a "Bonjour" before any other question or request.

If a man takes your hand be prepared for him, being polite, to kiss it. If you are a man and want to try this on a French woman, take her hand gently and kiss your own thumb. It is only when you know her well that you can really kiss her hand. This is a bit old fashioned but not extinct.

Table etiquette: a rule instilled in children. Hands should always be on the table, not underneath it. *(This also applies in Germany and most European countries as far as can be verified.)*
When asked if you would like a second helping, be careful. "Merci" can mean "No". It is better to say "Avec plaisir" or "Oui merci". *(In German, Danke – thank you means No so you must reply Ja bitte if you want something.)*
A traditional wedding present in France is a set of "porte couteau" made of glass, china or silver; a useful gadget to keep your knife for the next course.
If helping to lay the table note that the knife and fork are put on each side of the plate as in England but the dessertspoon and fork are put above the plate as in the British informal way.

Health by the sea
Suntan cream for full protection from the sun. Use a cream which has a high factor number e.g. Factor 50 as this protects against burning (UVB). To protect against aging and developing melanomas use a cream with a high UVA rating. It has five stars on the packaging. To protect the skin while in the water (especially for children) use a waterproof cream (strength indicated on the packaging). The stronger creams are thicker and last longer. The less strong, thinner creams need to be applied more often. Suntan creams available at Boots or any good pharmacy.
A light weight swim suit can be all in one, covering legs and arms or as shorts and a t-shirt. They are not as effective when wet so cream should be used as well. Towelling off will remove the cream so reapply it. For eczema sufferers use a rash vest under the wetsuit, obtainable from sports shops. These will also serve as sun protection.
For jelly fish stings use vinegar as opposed to sea urchin spine injuries which need bicarbonate of soda.

Glastonbury Festival – How to enjoy /survive it.
Glastonbury is not only for popular music. There are many other activities, a theatre, talks and lectures, a circus, a children's play area, crafts and hobby demonstrations, shops, banks and information on environmental issues. There is also a welcome and welfare centre run by Somerset Churches Together open all 24 hours for general help such as finding your 'blue tent', one of several thousands, and to provide temporary overnight shelter.

Regular worship (twice daily) is also available there besides pastoral care and counselling.

What to do if you are arrested
If you are told that you have to go to the police station but you "could just" or "it might be easier for you to" accept a caution, DON'T. This automatically gives you a permanent criminal record which prevents entry to the USA and rules out many positions and professions such as directorships, teaching, nursing, etc. Exercise your rights and ask for a solicitor to be present at the police station (this service is free for everyone).
The editor, when younger and late again, managed to climb up the side of a London bus. It is easy but doesn't get you there any earlier. No one was hurt.

TRAVELLING AND DRIVING

Travelling
In a **train**, sit facing rear, it is safer. A window seat avoids being hit by falling luggage.
By **air**, the tail end is safest. Window seats avoid falling luggage.
On board **ship**, in case of capsize the floor will become a wall. Note how fixed tables can act as a ladder. Sit near the exits. Travel by boat: In rough seas walk with legs wide apart to stabilize body.
Sea sickness: If known to be prone take an anti-sickness tablet such as Cinnarazine (Stugeron) in advance. If feeling mildly sick having a meal may help. Travelling in the centre of the boat gives less vertical and horizontal movement. Take some brandy. Stay in the open air or go quickly below and lie down in the dark. The editor, then an impoverished and very hungry student, was on a long North Sea crossing. She went on deck and made friends with a charming gentleman. Unfortunately just as he was going to propose lunch he went very green and all hopes of a meal that day disappeared. Sadly such travelling friendships may not be safe nowadays.
Travel by **car**: Take a small length of piping to fit over the handle of a wrench, giving more leverage.
Travel sickness: Travel in front and open the windows or lie down with your eyes closed. For a child have a bowl ready in case it is impossible to stop the vomiting. Attach chain trailing on ground at rear. This removes static but sometimes still works when the chain is broken so there may be a placebo effect. Take travel sickness pills.
Keep a small sewing kit in the car, also spare essential make up, small secateurs and a first aid kit.

Driving
To unlock car from a distance, put metal point of key against temple and click. *(It works!)*
Driving with your hands on the steering wheel at a quarter past nine or ten to two (as on a clock face) gives best control – <u>not</u> at the top of the wheel. Keep a baseball cap on the dashboard of the car for very low sun.
On long journeys, stop every 2 hours. Have a sleep or a short walk. If sleepy and unable to stop, open the windows wide and sing some hymns or

favourite songs. Remove your shoes. It is safer to stop briefly by the motorway, get out and exercise than to fall asleep at the wheel.
After an accident take photos of the damage and all the occupants (carry a disposable a camera or use a mobile phone).
Beware especially if a driver waves you into the fast lane. The driver in front may slam on his brakes and you are to blame for the collision. When the claim appears against your insurance there may suddenly be a lot of phantom passengers with whip-lash injuries.

Speed	Thinking Distance	Braking Distances	Stopping Distance
20 mph	20ft (6metres)	20ft (6 metres)	40ft (12 metres)
30 mph	30ft (9 metres)	45 ft (14 metres)	75ft (23 metres)

At 20 mph the stopping distance is x2 the speed. At 60 mph the stopping distance is x4 the speed. To be aware of speed say the speed aloud to yourself when in a speed limited zone. Use low gear in 30 or 20 mph zone. One in 3 accidents occur within 1 mile of home.
If the car falls into deep water – open windows slowly. Allow water to enter as high as possible then open door.
When buying a car it is said that men focus on the engine and mpg, women on the interior layout, the vanity mirror and storage space for essentials and whether the radio works. *(What sexism!)*

Horses on the road
Take great care when passing horses on the road, whether ridden or led. Pass at 5 mph giving the widest berth the road affords. Never pass a horse from behind when there is another vehicle approaching from the other direction.
You will not hear or see the scary object in the undergrowth but the horse may react before the rider can control him. An accident may not be the vehicle driver's fault but slow considerate driving could save the life of the horse or rider.
If cycling up behind a horse, be aware that neither the horse nor the rider may see or hear you approaching. Shout out or ring a bell from a distance to warn of your approach and pass slowly giving the horse a wide berth. Never approach a horse at speed on a bicycle in either direction.